Table of Contents

Chapter 1: Introduction to JavaScript in Gaming

1.1. The Role of JavaScript in Modern Game Development

JavaScript plays a pivotal role in modern game development, offering a versatile and accessible platform for creating interactive and engaging gaming experiences. As a client-side scripting language, it allows game developers to craft games that can be run directly in web browsers, making them widely accessible to users across various devices and platforms.

One of the key advantages of using JavaScript in game development is its compatibility with HTML5 and CSS, forming the foundation of web-based gaming. This trio of technologies provides the necessary tools for rendering graphics, handling user interactions, and managing game logic. As a result, JavaScript empowers developers to create games that can be easily distributed online without requiring users to install additional software or plugins.

JavaScript also boasts a vibrant and supportive community, with a plethora of libraries and frameworks designed specifically for game development. Popular choices like Phaser and Babylon.js offer powerful features and abstractions that simplify complex tasks such as rendering graphics, managing animations, and handling input.

Moreover, JavaScript is an ideal choice for cross-platform game development. With the help of frameworks like Electron, developers can package their JavaScript-based games into standalone desktop applications for Windows, macOS, and Linux. This flexibility allows for wider distribution and potential revenue streams through app stores and digital distribution platforms.

In the context of mobile gaming, JavaScript shines as well. Thanks to frameworks like Cordova and PhoneGap, developers can wrap their JavaScript games in native wrappers, making them accessible on iOS and Android devices. This approach leverages the same codebase across different mobile platforms, streamlining development efforts and reducing time-to-market.

Furthermore, JavaScript is well-suited for multiplayer and online gaming experiences. With the integration of WebSockets and server-side scripting, developers can create real-time, multiplayer games that provide engaging social interactions for players. This capability opens up opportunities for creating competitive and collaborative gaming experiences that extend beyond the single-player paradigm.

In summary, JavaScript's versatility, accessibility, and compatibility with other web technologies make it a powerful choice for modern game development. Its ability to create games for web browsers, desktop, and mobile platforms, coupled with a vibrant developer community, ensures that JavaScript will continue to play a prominent role in shaping the future of gaming. In the following sections of this chapter, we will delve deeper into the specific aspects of using JavaScript for game development, including syntax, tools, and best practices.

1.2. Comparing JavaScript with Other Game Development Languages

When considering game development, it's essential to evaluate JavaScript in comparison to other programming languages commonly used in the industry. Each language has its strengths and weaknesses, and the choice depends on various factors, including project requirements, target platforms, and developer expertise.

JavaScript vs. C++

One of the most significant comparisons in game development is between JavaScript and C++. C++ has been a staple in the industry for decades, primarily due to its raw performance and low-level control over hardware. Game engines like Unreal Engine and Unity use C++ extensively for their core components.

JavaScript, on the other hand, is a high-level, interpreted language. While it may not match C++ in terms of raw performance, it offers rapid development capabilities and is well-suited for web-based and cross-platform games. JavaScript's ease of use and the vast ecosystem of web technologies make it an attractive choice for smaller studios and indie developers.

JavaScript vs. C

C# is another language commonly used in game development, especially in the Unity game engine. Like JavaScript, C# offers high-level abstractions and productivity gains. It's known for its strong typing and garbage collection, which can simplify memory management compared to C++.

JavaScript, being a dynamically typed language, provides flexibility but may introduce runtime errors that are caught only during execution. While this can be a drawback, it also makes JavaScript more forgiving and approachable for beginners.

JavaScript vs. Python

Python is gaining popularity in the game development world, thanks to engines like Godot and frameworks like Pygame. Python's simplicity and readability make it an excellent choice for prototyping and smaller games. It has a robust community and extensive libraries for various tasks.

JavaScript shares some similarities with Python, such as dynamic typing and ease of use. However, JavaScript's strength in web-based gaming and browser compatibility gives it an edge for projects with a strong online or cross-platform focus.

JavaScript vs. Rust

Rust is an emerging language known for its memory safety guarantees and performance. While not as widely adopted as C++ or C#, it is gaining traction in the gaming industry.

Rust's focus on preventing common programming errors can lead to more stable and secure game code.

JavaScript, in contrast, may require extra care to manage memory efficiently and avoid memory leaks. However, its accessibility and the ability to harness the power of web technologies make it an appealing choice for web-based and mobile games.

In conclusion, the choice of programming language for game development depends on a variety of factors, including project goals, team expertise, and target platforms. JavaScript shines in web-based gaming, cross-platform development, and rapid prototyping, making it an excellent choice for many game developers, especially those looking to reach a broad audience and explore online multiplayer experiences.

1.3. Setting Up Your Development Environment

Before diving into JavaScript game development, it's crucial to set up a suitable development environment. A well-configured environment ensures that you can efficiently write, test, and debug your game code. Here are the key steps to set up your JavaScript game development environment:

Choose a Text Editor or Integrated Development Environment (IDE)

Selecting the right text editor or IDE is the first step. Some popular choices for JavaScript game development include Visual Studio Code, Sublime Text, Atom, and WebStorm. These tools offer features like syntax highlighting, code completion, and debugging support tailored for JavaScript.

Install Node.js and npm

Node.js is a runtime environment for executing JavaScript on the server side. It also includes npm (Node Package Manager) for managing JavaScript packages and libraries. Install Node.js and npm to access a vast ecosystem of JavaScript modules that can enhance your game development workflow.

To install Node.js and npm, visit the official website (https://nodejs.org/), download the installer for your platform, and follow the installation instructions.

Set Up a Version Control System

Using a version control system (VCS) is essential for tracking changes in your game's source code and collaborating with others. Git is a widely used VCS that integrates seamlessly with JavaScript development. Create a Git repository for your game project and commit your initial codebase.

Create a Project Structure

Organize your game project with a clear directory structure. Typically, you might have folders for assets (images, audio, and other resources), source code, libraries, and build output. A well-structured project makes it easier to manage and maintain your game.

Choose a Game Development Framework

Consider whether you want to build your game from scratch or leverage an existing game development framework or engine. Frameworks like Phaser, Three.js, and PixiJS provide pre-built components and utilities for common game development tasks, allowing you to focus on game-specific logic.

Set Up a Local Development Server

Many JavaScript games require a local development server to serve your game files, especially when working with web technologies. You can use tools like `http-server`, `express.js`, or Python's `http.server` for this purpose. Running a local server ensures that your game runs correctly with the same conditions as it would on a web server.

Configure Build and Compilation Tools

Depending on your game's complexity and requirements, you may need to set up build and compilation tools. Tools like Webpack, Babel, and TypeScript can help bundle and transpile your code for optimal performance and compatibility.

Install Browser Developer Tools

Web browsers offer developer tools that are indispensable for debugging JavaScript code. Familiarize yourself with the developer console, network inspector, and debugging features available in your chosen browser. These tools will help you identify and resolve issues in your game.

Test Across Multiple Browsers and Devices

Ensure your game is cross-browser and cross-device compatible. Test it on different web browsers (Chrome, Firefox, Safari, Edge, etc.) and various devices (desktop, tablet, mobile) to identify and address any compatibility issues.

Set Up Automated Testing and Continuous Integration (Optional)

For larger projects, consider implementing automated testing and continuous integration (CI) pipelines to catch bugs and ensure code quality. Tools like Jest, Mocha, and Travis CI can assist in this regard.

In conclusion, setting up your JavaScript game development environment is a crucial initial step. It lays the foundation for efficient and productive development. Take the time to configure your environment carefully, and you'll be well-prepared to start creating your JavaScript games.

1.4. Basic JavaScript Syntax and Concepts for Games

To get started with JavaScript game development, it's essential to have a solid grasp of basic JavaScript syntax and concepts. In this section, we'll cover some fundamental aspects of JavaScript that are particularly relevant to game development.

Variables and Data Types

JavaScript uses variables to store and manage data. Variables can hold various data types, including numbers, strings, booleans, arrays, and objects. Here's a quick overview of variable declaration and data types:

```javascript
// Variable declaration and assignment
let playerName = "John";
let score = 100;
let isActive = true;

// Arrays and objects
let inventory = ["sword", "shield", "potion"];
let playerInfo = {
  name: "Alice",
  health: 80,
  level: 3
};
```

Functions

Functions are reusable blocks of code that perform specific tasks. You can define your own functions or use built-in ones. Functions are essential for organizing and encapsulating game logic:

```javascript
// Defining a function
function calculateDamage(damageValue, armorValue) {
  return damageValue - armorValue;
}

// Calling a function
let finalDamage = calculateDamage(50, 10);
```

Conditional Statements

Conditional statements like if, else if, and else allow you to control the flow of your game based on certain conditions:

```javascript
let playerHealth = 75;

if (playerHealth > 0) {
```

```
  console.log("Player is alive");
} else {
  console.log("Player is defeated");
}
```

Loops

Loops like for and while are used for repeating actions multiple times. They're valuable for iterating through arrays or simulating game time:

```
// Using a for loop to iterate through an array
let enemies = ["goblin", "skeleton", "dragon"];
for (let i = 0; i < enemies.length; i++) {
  console.log("Enemy: " + enemies[i]);
}
```

Event Handling

In game development, you often need to respond to user input or events. JavaScript provides event listeners to capture and handle user interactions:

```
// Adding a click event listener
document.getElementById("start-button").addEventListener("click", function()
{
  startGame();
});
```

Classes and Object-Oriented Programming

JavaScript supports object-oriented programming (OOP) using classes and prototypes. This is useful for creating game objects with properties and methods:

```
// Creating a simple player class
class Player {
  constructor(name, health) {
    this.name = name;
    this.health = health;
  }

  attack() {
    console.log(`${this.name} attacks!`);
  }
}

let player1 = new Player("Alice", 100);
player1.attack();
```

DOM Manipulation

In web-based games, you'll often need to manipulate the Document Object Model (DOM) to update the game's user interface. JavaScript can be used to access and modify HTML elements:

```javascript
// Updating the game score in the DOM
let scoreElement = document.getElementById("score");
scoreElement.textContent = "Score: 150";
```

Game Loop

A game typically runs in a continuous loop to update game logic and render graphics. The game loop ensures that animations are smooth and responsive to user input:

```javascript
// Basic game loop structure
function gameLoop() {
  updateGameLogic();
  renderGraphics();
  requestAnimationFrame(gameLoop); // Continue the loop
}

gameLoop(); // Start the game loop
```

These are some of the essential JavaScript concepts you'll encounter in game development. Understanding these fundamentals is crucial as you progress to more advanced topics in JavaScript game development.

1.5. Understanding the Game Development Lifecycle

Understanding the game development lifecycle is crucial for building successful games in JavaScript. It involves a series of stages, each with its specific tasks and objectives. Here's an overview of the typical game development lifecycle:

1. Conceptualization

In this initial phase, you brainstorm and outline your game concept. Define the game's core mechanics, objectives, and target audience. Create a game design document (GDD) that outlines the game's story, characters, levels, and gameplay.

2. Pre-production

During pre-production, you plan the project's scope, budget, and timeline. Create a detailed project plan and assemble your development team if working with others. Develop a prototype or proof of concept to test the feasibility of your game idea.

3. Production

Production is where you start building the game. Write code, create game assets (art, audio, animations), and implement the game mechanics. Collaborate closely with artists, sound designers, and other team members to ensure the game's assets align with your vision.

```
// Example: Loading an image asset in JavaScript
const image = new Image();
image.src = "images/player.png";
```

4. Testing and Quality Assurance

Testing is a critical phase to identify and fix bugs and ensure the game's stability. Conduct playtesting to gather user feedback and make improvements based on player experiences. Test the game on different devices and browsers to ensure compatibility.

```
// Example: Adding a simple test function
function runTests() {
  // Your testing code here
}

runTests();
```

5. Alpha and Beta Testing

During alpha testing, the game is tested internally by your development team to catch major issues. Beta testing involves releasing a limited version to a select group of external testers or players. Collect feedback and address issues discovered during these phases.

6. Polishing

The polishing phase involves refining the game's graphics, animations, and user interface. Make any necessary adjustments based on player feedback and testing results. Optimize performance to ensure smooth gameplay.

```
// Example: Optimizing code for better performance
function optimizeGame() {
  // Your optimization code here
}

optimizeGame();
```

7. Localization and Accessibility

If your game targets a global audience, consider localization by translating the game into multiple languages. Ensure accessibility features are implemented to make the game accessible to players with disabilities.

8. Marketing and Promotion

Develop a marketing strategy to promote your game. Create a website, engage with social media, and reach out to gaming communities and influencers. Build anticipation for your game's release.

```javascript
// Example: Using JavaScript to integrate social media sharing
function shareOnSocialMedia() {
    // Your sharing code here
}

shareOnSocialMedia();
```

9. Release

Launch your game on the chosen platforms or distribution channels. Coordinate release dates and times to maximize visibility. Monitor player feedback and be prepared to address any post-launch issues quickly.

10. Post-launch Support and Updates

After the game is released, continue to support it with updates, bug fixes, and additional content. Engage with the player community, listen to their feedback, and consider their suggestions for future improvements.

```javascript
// Example: Updating the game with new features
function updateGame() {
    // Your update code here
}

updateGame();
```

11. Monetization and Analytics

Implement monetization strategies, such as ads, in-app purchases, or premium features. Integrate analytics tools to track player behavior, engagement, and revenue. Use this data to make informed decisions and optimize your game.

Understanding and following this game development lifecycle helps you stay organized and ensures that your JavaScript game is developed efficiently and effectively. Each stage contributes to the overall success of your game, from the initial concept to post-launch support and beyond.

Chapter 2: Graphics and Animation Basics

2.1. Introduction to Canvas API

The Canvas API is a fundamental tool for rendering graphics and creating animations in JavaScript games. It provides a way to draw 2D graphics directly within an HTML5 <canvas> element. This section introduces you to the Canvas API and how to get started with it.

Creating a Canvas Element

To use the Canvas API, you need an HTML <canvas> element in your web page. You can create a canvas element like this:

```
<canvas id="gameCanvas" width="800" height="600"></canvas>
```

Here, we've created a canvas with an id of "gameCanvas" and specified its width and height. These dimensions determine the size of the drawing surface.

Accessing the Canvas Context

To draw on the canvas, you'll need to access its rendering context. You can do this using JavaScript:

```
const canvas = document.getElementById("gameCanvas");
const context = canvas.getContext("2d");
```

The getContext("2d") method returns a 2D rendering context. This context provides methods and properties for drawing shapes, text, and images on the canvas.

Drawing Shapes

The Canvas API allows you to draw various shapes, including rectangles, circles, lines, and paths. Here's an example of drawing a filled rectangle:

```
context.fillStyle = "blue"; // Set fill color to blue
context.fillRect(50, 50, 100, 100); // Draw a filled rectangle
```

In this example, we set the fill color to blue using fillStyle and then use fillRect to draw a filled rectangle at coordinates (50, 50) with a width and height of 100 pixels.

Drawing Images

You can also draw images on the canvas, which is essential for creating game sprites and backgrounds. To load and draw an image, you can use the following code:

```
const image = new Image();
image.src = "image.png"; // Replace with your image file path

image.onload = function() {
```

```
  context.drawImage(image, 0, 0); // Draw the image at (0, 0)
};
```

Here, we create an `Image` object, set its source using `src`, and then use `drawImage` to render the image at the specified coordinates (0, 0).

For smooth animations, it's best to use the `requestAnimationFrame` method to update and redraw your canvas continuously. Here's a simplified example of an animation loop:

```
function animate() {
    // Update game logic here

    // Clear the canvas
    context.clearRect(0, 0, canvas.width, canvas.height);

    // Draw game objects here

    requestAnimationFrame(animate);
}

// Start the animation loop
animate();
```

In the `animate` function, you update your game logic, clear the canvas using `clearRect`, draw your game objects, and then call `requestAnimationFrame` to schedule the next frame.

These are the basic concepts of working with the Canvas API in JavaScript for game development. In the following sections, we'll explore more advanced graphics and animation techniques to enhance your games.

2.2. Rendering Shapes and Images

In JavaScript game development, rendering shapes and images on the canvas is a fundamental part of creating interactive and visually appealing games. This section explores the techniques for rendering various shapes and images using the Canvas API.

Drawing Basic Shapes

Rectangles

Rectangles are one of the most commonly used shapes in game development. You can draw rectangles on the canvas using `fillRect` and `strokeRect` methods. Here's an example of drawing a filled and a stroked rectangle:

```
// Filled rectangle
context.fillStyle = "blue";
context.fillRect(50, 50, 100, 100);

// Stroked rectangle
context.strokeStyle = "red";
context.lineWidth = 4;
context.strokeRect(200, 50, 100, 100);
```

In this code, we first draw a filled blue rectangle and then a red stroked rectangle.

Circles

To draw circles, you can use the `arc` method. Here's an example of drawing a filled circle:

```
context.beginPath();
context.arc(150, 150, 50, 0, Math.PI * 2); // (x, y, radius, startAngle, endAngle)
context.fillStyle = "green";
context.fill();
```

The `arc` method creates a path for a circle with the specified center (150, 150), radius (50), and angles to define a complete circle. We then set the fill color to green and fill the circle.

Drawing Images

Loading Images

Loading and rendering images is essential for creating game sprites and backgrounds. To load an image, you can use the `Image` object as shown earlier. Here's how to load an image and draw it on the canvas:

```
const image = new Image();
image.src = "image.png"; // Replace with your image file path

image.onload = function() {
  context.drawImage(image, 50, 50); // Draw the image at (50, 50)
};
```

This code loads an image, specifies its source using `src`, and uses the `drawImage` method to render it on the canvas.

Scaling and Transforming Images

You can scale and transform images using the `drawImage` method. This is useful for resizing, rotating, or flipping sprites:

```
// Scaling an image
context.drawImage(image, 0, 0, 100, 100); // Draw a 100x100 version of the image
```

```
// Transforming an image (scaling and rotation)
context.setTransform(1, 0, 0, 1, 0, 0); // Reset the transformation matrix
context.translate(200, 200); // Translate to (200, 200)
context.rotate(Math.PI / 4); // Rotate by 45 degrees
context.drawImage(image, -50, -50, 100, 100); // Draw a rotated and scaled im
age
```

In this example, we first scale the image to 100x100 pixels. Then, we reset the transformation matrix, translate to a new position (200, 200), rotate the context by 45 degrees, and draw the image.

Working with Paths

The Canvas API also allows you to create custom shapes and paths. You can define paths using various drawing commands and then fill or stroke them.

```
// Creating a path for a triangle
context.beginPath();
context.moveTo(300, 150); // Move to the starting point
context.lineTo(400, 250); // Draw a line to the next point
context.lineTo(200, 250); // Draw another line
context.closePath(); // Close the path to complete the triangle
context.fillStyle = "yellow";
context.fill(); // Fill the triangle with yellow
```

In this code, we create a path for a triangle by specifying the vertices using moveTo and lineTo. We then close the path and fill it with a yellow color.

These are some of the essential techniques for rendering shapes and images in JavaScript game development using the Canvas API. By mastering these basics, you'll be well-prepared to create engaging visual elements for your games.

2.3. Basics of Animation with JavaScript

Animation is a crucial aspect of game development that brings life and interactivity to your games. JavaScript provides the tools and techniques to create animations, making your games more engaging and visually appealing. In this section, we'll explore the basics of animation in JavaScript games.

Animation Frames and requestAnimationFrame

To create animations, you'll need to update the canvas regularly to display different frames of your game. JavaScript provides the requestAnimationFrame method, which is a more efficient way to schedule animations compared to using setInterval or setTimeout.

Here's a simplified example of using requestAnimationFrame for animation:

```
function animate() {
  // Update game logic
  // ...

  // Clear the canvas
  context.clearRect(0, 0, canvas.width, canvas.height);

  // Draw game objects
  // ...

  // Request the next animation frame
  requestAnimationFrame(animate);
}

// Start the animation loop
animate();
```

In this code, the animate function is called repeatedly using requestAnimationFrame, creating a smooth animation loop. You update your game logic, clear the canvas to prepare for the next frame, and then draw your game objects. This loop continues until you decide to stop it.

Timing and Delta Time

For animations to run smoothly across different devices and frame rates, it's essential to consider timing. One common technique is to use delta time (often denoted as deltaTime or dt) to ensure that animations are frame rate independent.

Here's a basic example of using delta time in an animation loop:

```
let lastTime = 0;

function animate(currentTime) {
  const deltaTime = (currentTime - lastTime) / 1000; // Convert to seconds
  lastTime = currentTime;

  // Update game logic based on deltaTime
  // ...

  // Clear the canvas
  context.clearRect(0, 0, canvas.width, canvas.height);

  // Draw game objects
  // ...

  // Request the next animation frame
  requestAnimationFrame(animate);
}
```

```
// Start the animation loop
animate();
```

In this code, we calculate the time elapsed between frames using `deltaTime`. You can then use `deltaTime` to update your game logic, ensuring that movements and animations are consistent regardless of the frame rate.

Tweening and Interpolation

Tweening (short for "in-betweening") is a common animation technique used to create smooth transitions between different states or positions. It's especially useful for animating object movements, fades, and transitions.

JavaScript libraries like Tween.js or GreenSock Animation Platform (GSAP) provide easy-to-use functions for tweening properties over time. Here's a simplified example using GSAP to tween an object's position:

```
// Import GSAP library (ensure it's loaded in your HTML)
// <script src="https://cdnjs.cloudflare.com/ajax/libs/gsap/3.10.1/gsap.min.j
s"></script>

const box = document.getElementById("animatedBox");

gsap.to(box, {
  duration: 2, // Animation duration in seconds
  x: 200,      // Target x-coordinate
  y: 300,      // Target y-coordinate
  ease: "power2.inOut", // Easing function
  repeat: -1, // Repeat the animation indefinitely
  yoyo: true  // Reverse the animation on each repeat
});
```

In this example, we use GSAP to animate the position of an HTML element with the id "animatedBox" to (200, 300) over a duration of 2 seconds, applying easing and repeating the animation indefinitely with a yoyo effect.

These are some of the fundamental concepts and techniques for creating animations in JavaScript games. Animation is a vast topic, and as you progress in game development, you can explore more advanced animations, including sprite animations, particle effects, and character animations.

2.4. Creating Sprites and Sprite Animations

In game development, sprites are 2D images or animations that represent game objects, characters, items, or enemies. They are a fundamental element for rendering objects on the

37

screen. This section explores the concept of sprites and how to create sprite animations in JavaScript games.

Understanding Sprites

Sprites are typically 2D images or animations with transparent backgrounds that can be placed anywhere on the game canvas. They are used to depict game characters, objects, or effects. Each sprite is associated with a specific image file or sprite sheet containing multiple frames.

Using Sprite Sheets

Sprite sheets are a common technique for managing and animating sprites efficiently. A sprite sheet is a single image file that contains multiple frames or animations of a sprite. By selecting specific regions of the sprite sheet, you can display different frames to create animations.

Here's an example of a sprite sheet and how to use it in JavaScript:

```javascript
// Load the sprite sheet image
const spriteSheet = new Image();
spriteSheet.src = "spritesheet.png";

// Define a sprite object with frame coordinates
const sprite = {
  sheet: spriteSheet,
  frameWidth: 64,
  frameHeight: 64,
  frameCount: 8,
  currentFrame: 0,
};

// Draw the current frame of the sprite
context.drawImage(
  sprite.sheet,
  sprite.currentFrame * sprite.frameWidth,
  0, // Assuming the sprite is in the top row
  sprite.frameWidth,
  sprite.frameHeight,
  x, // Destination x-coordinate on the canvas
  y, // Destination y-coordinate on the canvas
  sprite.frameWidth,
  sprite.frameHeight
);
```

In this code, we load a sprite sheet image and define a sprite object with frame information. We then use the drawImage method to display the current frame of the sprite on the canvas. By updating sprite.currentFrame, you can animate the sprite by changing the displayed frame.

Creating Sprite Animations

To create sprite animations, you need to update the `currentFrame` property of the sprite object over time. You can achieve this by incrementing the frame index at a specific rate, creating the illusion of motion.

Here's a simplified example of creating a sprite animation loop:

```
const animationSpeed = 100; // Milliseconds per frame

function animateSprite() {
  sprite.currentFrame = (sprite.currentFrame + 1) % sprite.frameCount;
  context.clearRect(0, 0, canvas.width, canvas.height);
  context.drawImage(
    sprite.sheet,
    sprite.currentFrame * sprite.frameWidth,
    0, // Assuming the sprite is in the top row
    sprite.frameWidth,
    sprite.frameHeight,
    x, // Destination x-coordinate on the canvas
    y, // Destination y-coordinate on the canvas
    sprite.frameWidth,
    sprite.frameHeight
  );
  setTimeout(animateSprite, animationSpeed);
}

// Start the animation loop
animateSprite();
```

In this example, the `animateSprite` function increments the `currentFrame` and redraws the sprite at the specified rate, creating a continuous animation loop.

Handling Sprite Collisions and Interactions

Sprites are not only for animation but also for game interactions. You can implement collision detection between sprites and respond to events like sprite interactions, attacks, or power-ups.

Here's a basic example of collision detection between two sprites:

```
function checkCollision(spriteA, spriteB) {
  const rectA = {
    x: spriteA.x,
    y: spriteA.y,
    width: spriteA.frameWidth,
    height: spriteA.frameHeight,
  };

  const rectB = {
    x: spriteB.x,
```

```
    y: spriteB.y,
    width: spriteB.frameWidth,
    height: spriteB.frameHeight,
  };

  return (
    rectA.x < rectB.x + rectB.width &&
    rectA.x + rectA.width > rectB.x &&
    rectA.y < rectB.y + rectB.height &&
    rectA.y + rectA.height > rectB.y
  );
}

// Example usage
if (checkCollision(sprite1, sprite2)) {
  // Handle the collision between sprite1 and sprite2
}
```

In this code, checkCollision checks if two sprites, spriteA and spriteB, are colliding by comparing their bounding rectangles. If a collision is detected, you can implement specific actions or behaviors for the sprites.

Sprites play a fundamental role in game development, allowing you to create visually appealing animations and interactions. By mastering the concepts of sprite sheets, animations, and collision detection, you can bring your game characters and objects to life.

2.5. Implementing Parallax Effects

Parallax effects are a visually captivating technique used in game development to create depth and immersion in 2D games. This section explores the concept of parallax scrolling and how to implement it in JavaScript games.

Understanding Parallax Scrolling

Parallax scrolling is a technique where multiple layers of background images move at different speeds as the player navigates through the game world. This creates an illusion of depth and adds a dynamic element to the game's environment.

In a typical parallax setup, there are multiple layers or "parallax planes." The foreground planes move faster than the background planes, creating a sense of perspective. This effect is commonly used to simulate scrolling in side-scrolling games or to add dimension to top-down games.

Implementing Parallax Scrolling

To implement parallax scrolling in JavaScript games, you need to move the background layers at different speeds relative to the camera or player's movement. Here's a basic example of how to achieve parallax scrolling:

```javascript
// Define parallax layers with their properties
const parallaxLayers = [
  { image: "background1.jpg", speed: 0.2 },
  { image: "background2.jpg", speed: 0.5 },
  { image: "foreground1.png", speed: 1.0 },
  // Add more layers as needed
];

// Load images for each layer
const images = [];
parallaxLayers.forEach(layer => {
  const image = new Image();
  image.src = layer.image;
  images.push(image);
});

// Draw the parallax layers based on player's position
function drawParallaxLayers(playerX) {
  context.clearRect(0, 0, canvas.width, canvas.height);

  parallaxLayers.forEach(layer => {
    const offsetX = playerX * layer.speed;
    context.drawImage(images[parallaxLayers.indexOf(layer)], -offsetX, 0);
  });

  // Draw game objects on top of the parallax layers
  // ...
}

// Update the player's position and redraw the layers
function updateGame(playerX) {
  // Update player's position and game logic
  // ...

  // Redraw parallax layers based on player's position
  drawParallaxLayers(playerX);

  // Draw game objects on top of the parallax layers
  // ...

  requestAnimationFrame(() => updateGame(playerX));
}
```

```
// Start the game loop with an initial player position
updateGame(initialPlayerX);
```

In this code, we define an array of parallax layers with their images and speeds. We load the images and then use the `drawParallaxLayers` function to draw the layers based on the player's position. The layers move at different speeds, creating a parallax effect.

Customizing Parallax Layers

You can customize the number and properties of parallax layers to achieve the desired visual effect. Adjusting layer speeds, adding more layers, or using images with varying dimensions can create unique parallax scrolling experiences.

Parallax Effects in Different Game Types

Parallax scrolling is versatile and can be applied to various game types, including platformers, shooters, and adventure games. By adapting the parallax layers and their speeds to fit the game's theme and environment, you can enhance the player's immersion and enjoyment.

Implementing parallax effects in your JavaScript games adds depth and visual appeal, making the game world feel more dynamic and engaging. Experiment with different layer arrangements and speeds to achieve the desired parallax effect for your game.

Chapter 3: Game Logic and Flow Control

3.1. Structuring Game Code

Structuring your game code is crucial for maintaining a well-organized and maintainable project. In this section, we'll explore various techniques and patterns for structuring your game code effectively.

The Importance of Code Structure

As your game project grows, maintaining a clear and organized codebase becomes essential. A well-structured codebase is easier to debug, extend, and collaborate on with other developers. It also helps you avoid common pitfalls like code duplication, tight coupling, and spaghetti code.

Modularization

One of the fundamental principles in code structuring is modularization. Break your game code into separate modules or files, each responsible for a specific aspect of the game. For example, you might have modules for player controls, enemy behavior, rendering, and sound management.

Here's a simple example of how you can structure your game code using ES6 modules:

```
// player.js - Player character module
export class Player {
  constructor() {
    // Initialize player properties
  }

  // Player methods
  move() {
    // Handle player movement
  }

  attack() {
    // Handle player attacks
  }
}

// enemy.js - Enemy behavior module
export class Enemy {
  constructor() {
    // Initialize enemy properties
  }

  // Enemy methods
  move() {
```

```
  // Handle enemy movement
  }

  attack() {
    // Handle enemy attacks
  }
}
```

By breaking down your game into modules, you encapsulate related functionality and make it easier to manage and extend each part of the game.

Game Loop

The game loop is a critical component of structuring game code. It controls the flow of the game by repeatedly updating the game state and rendering frames. The game loop typically consists of the following steps:

1. Input Handling: Collect and process user input (e.g., keyboard or mouse events).
2. Update: Update the game state, including player positions, enemy behavior, and game logic.
3. Render: Draw the game objects and backgrounds on the canvas.
4. Repeat: Repeat the loop to create an ongoing game experience.

Here's a simplified example of a game loop structure:

```
function gameLoop() {
    // Input handling
    handleInput();

    // Update game state
    updateGameState();

    // Render the game
    renderGame();

    // Repeat the loop
    requestAnimationFrame(gameLoop);
}

// Start the game loop
gameLoop();
```

This structure ensures that your game logic remains synchronized with the screen's refresh rate, providing a smooth gaming experience.

Entity-Component System (ECS)

In more complex games, you may encounter the need for an entity-component system (ECS) architecture. ECS is a design pattern that allows you to compose game objects (entities) from reusable components.

In an ECS, game entities are composed of various components, each responsible for a specific aspect of behavior or data. For example, you might have components for position, rendering, physics, and AI. This separation of concerns makes it easier to create diverse and complex game objects.

Here's a simplified example of how an ECS might look in JavaScript:

```javascript
// Entity.js - Game entity definition
export class Entity {
  constructor() {
    this.components = [];
  }

  addComponent(component) {
    this.components.push(component);
  }

  // Entity methods for component management
}

// Component.js - Base component class
export class Component {
  constructor() {
    // Initialize component properties
  }

  // Component methods
}

// Example components (e.g., PositionComponent, RenderComponent, AIComponent)
```

ECS can provide a scalable and flexible way to structure game code, especially for games with many different types of entities and behaviors.

Summary

Structuring game code is a critical aspect of game development. By following principles like modularization, implementing a well-organized game loop, and considering more advanced patterns like ECS, you can create maintainable and extensible game projects. Good code structure simplifies debugging, enhances collaboration, and ultimately contributes to the success of your game.

3.2. Event Handling and Input Control

In game development, event handling and input control play a pivotal role in making games interactive and responsive to player actions. This section explores how to effectively handle user input and events in JavaScript games.

The Role of Event Handling

Event handling is the process of capturing and responding to various events triggered by user actions or system interactions. In a game, events can encompass a wide range of actions, such as mouse clicks, keyboard inputs, touch gestures, and gamepad interactions. Proper event handling allows your game to interpret these actions and respond accordingly.

Handling Keyboard Input

Keyboard input is a fundamental way for players to control characters and interact with the game world. JavaScript provides event listeners to capture keyboard events like keydown, keyup, and keypress.

Here's a basic example of how to handle keyboard input in JavaScript:

```
// Add a keydown event listener to the document
document.addEventListener("keydown", function(event) {
  // Check the keyCode or key property to identify the pressed key
  if (event.keyCode === 37 || event.key === "ArrowLeft") {
    // Handle left arrow key press (e.g., move player left)
  } else if (event.keyCode === 39 || event.key === "ArrowRight") {
    // Handle right arrow key press (e.g., move player right)
  }
  // Add more key handling as needed
});
```

In this code, we listen for keydown events and check the keyCode or key property to identify which key was pressed. You can then perform game-specific actions based on the key input.

Handling Mouse Events

Mouse events are essential for interactions like clicking on objects, buttons, or elements within the game. JavaScript provides event listeners for mouse events such as click, mousedown, mouseup, mousemove, and more.

Here's a simple example of handling a mouse click event in JavaScript:

```
// Add a click event listener to a canvas element
canvas.addEventListener("click", function(event) {
  const mouseX = event.clientX - canvas.getBoundingClientRect().left;
  const mouseY = event.clientY - canvas.getBoundingClientRect().top;

  // Check if the mouse click occurred on a specific game object
```

```
  if (isClickInsideObject(mouseX, mouseY, gameObject)) {
    // Handle the click event (e.g., interact with the object)
  }
});
```

In this code, we calculate the mouse coordinates relative to the canvas element and check if the click occurred inside a specific game object. This allows you to trigger actions or interactions based on mouse clicks.

Handling Touch and Gesture Events

For mobile games and touch-enabled devices, touch and gesture events are crucial. JavaScript provides event listeners for touchstart, touchmove, touchend, and gesture events.

Here's a simplified example of handling a touch event in JavaScript:

```
// Add a touchstart event listener to a canvas element
canvas.addEventListener("touchstart", function(event) {
  const touchX = event.touches[0].clientX - canvas.getBoundingClientRect().left;
  const touchY = event.touches[0].clientY - canvas.getBoundingClientRect().top;

  // Handle the touch event (e.g., touch-based controls)
});
```

In this code, we extract the touch coordinates and handle the touch event accordingly. You can implement touch-based controls, gestures, and interactions to enhance the mobile gaming experience.

Handling Gamepad Input

For games played on platforms with gamepad support, such as consoles or PC controllers, you can also handle gamepad input in JavaScript. The Gamepad API provides events and information about connected gamepads and their inputs.

Here's a basic example of handling gamepad input:

```
// Check for connected gamepads
function checkGamepads() {
  const gamepads = navigator.getGamepads();

  for (const gamepad of gamepads) {
    if (gamepad) {
      // Handle gamepad button presses and joystick inputs
      // ...
    }
  }
}
```

```
// Periodically check for gamepad input (e.g., in the game loop)
setInterval(checkGamepads, 100);
```

In this code, we periodically check for connected gamepads and handle button presses and joystick inputs. The Gamepad API provides information about button states, joystick positions, and more.

Summary

Effective event handling and input control are essential for creating responsive and interactive games in JavaScript. Whether you're dealing with keyboard, mouse, touch, or gamepad input, understanding how to capture and process events allows you to create engaging gameplay experiences. By incorporating event handling into your game code, you can respond to player actions and make your games come to life.

3.3. Implementing Game Loops

A game loop is the heart of any real-time game, responsible for updating game logic and rendering frames at a consistent rate. In this section, we'll delve into the concept of game loops and how to implement them effectively in JavaScript games.

The Purpose of a Game Loop

A game loop serves several critical purposes in game development:

1. **Updating Game Logic:** It ensures that the game's logic, including player movements, enemy behavior, and game state, is updated at a consistent rate. This maintains game consistency across different devices and frame rates.

2. **Rendering Frames:** The loop renders frames to the screen, creating the illusion of animation and continuous gameplay. It ensures that the game's visuals are refreshed frequently enough to provide smooth motion.

3. **Synchronization:** It synchronizes the game's actions with the refresh rate of the display (usually 60 frames per second or FPS). This synchronization ensures that the game runs at a uniform pace on various devices.

The Basic Structure of a Game Loop

A game loop typically consists of three essential parts:

1. **Input Handling:** In this phase, the game captures player inputs, such as keyboard presses, mouse clicks, or touch events. It processes these inputs to determine how the game should respond.

2. **Update Logic:** This phase updates the game state, including player positions, enemy actions, physics calculations, and any other dynamic aspects of the game. It advances the game's logic based on the time elapsed since the previous frame.

3. **Rendering:** In this phase, the game draws the updated game objects and backgrounds to the screen. It refreshes the screen with the current frame's visuals.

Here's a simplified example of a game loop structure in JavaScript:

```javascript
function gameLoop() {
  // Input handling
  handleInput();

  // Update game logic
  updateGameState();

  // Render the game
  renderGame();

  // Request the next frame
  requestAnimationFrame(gameLoop);
}

// Start the game loop
gameLoop();
```

In this code, the requestAnimationFrame function is used to create a loop that calls gameLoop repeatedly. This ensures that the game loop runs at the screen's refresh rate.

Timing and Frame Rate Independence

To create a robust game loop, it's essential to account for variations in frame rate across different devices. Frame rate independence ensures that the game runs smoothly regardless of whether it's running on a high-end gaming PC or a mobile device.

One common technique for frame rate independence is using delta time (often denoted as deltaTime or dt). Delta time represents the time elapsed since the previous frame and is used to scale all time-based calculations.

Here's an example of incorporating delta time into a game loop:

```javascript
let lastTime = 0;

function gameLoop(currentTime) {
  const deltaTime = (currentTime - lastTime) / 1000; // Convert to seconds
  lastTime = currentTime;

  // Input handling
  handleInput();
```

```
// Update game logic based on deltaTime
updateGameState(deltaTime);

// Render the game
renderGame();

// Request the next frame
requestAnimationFrame(gameLoop);
}

// Start the game loop
gameLoop();
```

In this code, we calculate the `deltaTime` based on the time elapsed since the previous frame and pass it to the `updateGameState` function. This ensures that game logic updates are frame rate independent.

Fixed vs. Variable Time Step

Game loops can use either a fixed or variable time step approach. In a fixed time step, updates occur at a consistent time interval, ensuring that game logic behaves predictably. However, it may lead to stuttering if the frame rate drops significantly.

In a variable time step, updates occur based on the actual time passed since the last frame. This approach provides smoother gameplay but can introduce variability in game behavior.

The choice between fixed and variable time step depends on the specific requirements of your game. Action-packed games often favor variable time steps for smoother animation, while turn-based games may opt for fixed time steps for consistent gameplay.

Summary

A well-implemented game loop is essential for creating responsive and engaging games in JavaScript. By structuring your game around a game loop that handles input, updates game logic, and renders frames efficiently, you can provide a consistent and enjoyable gaming experience. Incorporating timing mechanisms like delta time ensures that your game runs smoothly across different devices and frame rates.

3.4. Collision Detection Basics

Collision detection is a fundamental aspect of game development, allowing games to detect and respond to interactions between game objects. In this section, we'll explore the basics of collision detection in JavaScript games.

The Importance of Collision Detection

Collision detection is essential for a wide range of game scenarios:

1. **Player-Object Interaction:** It enables players to interact with the game world by colliding with objects, picking up items, or triggering events.

2. **Enemy Behavior:** Collision detection helps determine if enemies collide with the player or other game objects, allowing you to implement behaviors like enemy attacks or enemy-player interactions.

3. **Obstacle Avoidance:** Games often require characters or objects to navigate around obstacles, which relies on detecting collisions with those obstacles.

4. **Projectile Collisions:** In shooting games, projectiles like bullets must detect collisions with enemies or obstacles to inflict damage or create impact effects.

Bounding Boxes and Collision Shapes

In collision detection, game objects are typically represented by bounding boxes or collision shapes. These shapes are simplified representations that encapsulate the object's area. Common collision shapes include:

- **Rectangles:** Used for objects with simple rectangular or square shapes.
- **Circles:** Useful for objects with circular or spherical shapes.
- **Polygons:** Can be used to represent more complex object shapes.

Collision shapes are often defined by their position (usually the object's center), dimensions, and sometimes additional properties like rotation. The choice of collision shape depends on the object's shape and complexity.

Overlapping and Separating Axis Theorem (SAT)

One common technique for collision detection is the Separating Axis Theorem (SAT). SAT checks for collisions by determining whether there exists a separating axis between two objects' collision shapes. If no separating axis is found, the objects are colliding.

Here's a simplified example of how SAT can be applied to collision detection between two rectangles:

```javascript
function areRectanglesColliding(rectA, rectB) {
  // Calculate the half-width and half-height of each rectangle
  const halfWidthA = rectA.width / 2;
  const halfHeightA = rectA.height / 2;
  const halfWidthB = rectB.width / 2;
  const halfHeightB = rectB.height / 2;

  // Calculate the centers of each rectangle
  const centerXA = rectA.x + halfWidthA;
  const centerYA = rectA.y + halfHeightA;
```

```
const centerXB = rectB.x + halfWidthB;
const centerYB = rectB.y + halfHeightB;

// Calculate the distance between the centers along both axes
const deltaX = Math.abs(centerXA - centerXB);
const deltaY = Math.abs(centerYA - centerYB);

// Check for overlap along both axes
if (deltaX < halfWidthA + halfWidthB && deltaY < halfHeightA + halfHeightB)
{
    // Rectangles are colliding
    return true;
}

// No overlap found
return false;
}
```

In this code, we calculate the half-width and half-height of each rectangle and then determine the distance between their centers along both the x and y axes. If the distances are smaller than the combined half-widths and half-heights, the rectangles are colliding.

Optimizing Collision Detection

Collision detection can be computationally expensive, especially in games with many objects. To optimize collision detection, consider using techniques like spatial partitioning (e.g., quadtree or grid-based systems) to reduce the number of collision checks between objects that are far apart. Additionally, implementing broad-phase and narrow-phase collision detection can help further optimize performance.

Summary

Collision detection is a fundamental concept in game development, allowing games to respond to interactions between game objects. By representing objects with collision shapes and applying techniques like the Separating Axis Theorem (SAT), you can detect collisions efficiently. Optimizing collision detection through spatial partitioning and other techniques is essential for maintaining smooth gameplay in complex games.

3.5. State Management in Games

State management is a crucial aspect of game development, as it helps control the flow and behavior of a game. In this section, we'll explore the significance of state management and how to effectively implement it in JavaScript games.

The Role of State Management

In game development, a "state" represents a specific condition or mode that the game can be in. Examples of game states include the main menu, gameplay, pause menu, game over screen, and victory screen. State management involves controlling transitions between these states and managing the behavior and data associated with each state.

Benefits of State Management

Effective state management offers several advantages:

1. **Organization:** It helps keep your code organized by separating different aspects of the game into distinct states. Each state can have its own logic, rendering, and input handling.

2. **Maintainability:** State management simplifies the process of adding, removing, or modifying game states. This makes it easier to expand your game or fix bugs related to specific states.

3. **Flexibility:** You can easily switch between different game states, allowing you to implement features like menus, cutscenes, and level transitions seamlessly.

4. **Efficiency:** By activating and deactivating states when necessary, you can optimize performance and reduce unnecessary processing.

Implementing State Management

To implement state management in JavaScript games, you can follow these general steps:

1. **Define Game States:** Identify the various states your game will have, such as "menu," "gameplay," "pause," and others. Each state should have its own logic, rendering, and input handling.

2. **State Stack:** Maintain a stack or list of active states. The top state on the stack is the current active state.

3. **State Transition:** Implement functions to push, pop, or switch between states. For example, when the player starts a new game, you may push the "gameplay" state onto the stack.

4. **Update and Render:** In the game loop, update and render the current active state. The active state's logic should control the game's behavior during that state.

Here's a simplified example of implementing state management in JavaScript:

```javascript
// Define game states as objects with update and render methods
const gameState = {
  name: "Gameplay",
  update: function() {
    // Update gameplay logic
  },
```

```javascript
  render: function() {
    // Render gameplay visuals
  },
};

const menuState = {
  name: "Menu",
  update: function() {
    // Update menu logic
  },
  render: function() {
    // Render menu visuals
  },
};

// Initialize a state stack with the initial state (e.g., menu)
const stateStack = [menuState];

// Game Loop
function gameLoop() {
  const currentState = stateStack[stateStack.length - 1]; // Get the top state

  currentState.update(); // Update the active state
  currentState.render(); // Render the active state
  requestAnimationFrame(gameLoop);
}

// Transition to a different state (e.g., gameplay)
function switchToGameplay() {
  stateStack.pop(); // Remove the current state (menu)
  stateStack.push(gameState); // Push the new state (gameplay)
}

// Start the game loop
gameLoop();
```

In this example, we define two game states, "Gameplay" and "Menu," and manage them using a state stack. By pushing and popping states onto the stack, you can easily switch between different game modes.

Using State Management for Menus

State management is particularly valuable for creating menus in games. You can have separate states for the main menu, options menu, pause menu, and other menu screens. When the player navigates through menus or starts a game, you can transition between these states seamlessly.

Summary

State management is a critical component of game development, allowing you to control the flow and behavior of your game. By defining and managing different game states, you can organize your code, improve maintainability, and implement various features and transitions effectively. Whether you're creating menus, gameplay modes, or cutscenes, state management helps you build a structured and engaging gaming experience in JavaScript.

Chapter 4: Advanced Graphics and Effects

4.1. Exploring WebGL for 3D Graphics

WebGL (Web Graphics Library) is a JavaScript API for rendering interactive 3D graphics within web browsers. In this section, we'll dive into the world of WebGL and understand how it can be leveraged for advanced 3D graphics in JavaScript games.

The Power of WebGL

WebGL unlocks the capability to create immersive 3D environments and stunning visuals directly in web browsers. It provides access to the GPU (Graphics Processing Unit), enabling real-time rendering of 3D scenes, complex animations, and special effects. WebGL is based on OpenGL ES, a widely used graphics API, making it a robust choice for game developers.

Key Features of WebGL

1. Hardware Acceleration:

WebGL harnesses the power of the GPU, allowing for fast and efficient rendering of 3D graphics. This results in smoother animations and improved performance, especially in graphics-intensive games.

2. Cross-Platform Compatibility:

WebGL is supported by major web browsers, including Chrome, Firefox, Safari, and Edge, making it a cross-platform solution for delivering 3D graphics on various devices.

3. Low-Level Graphics Control:

Developers have fine-grained control over the graphics pipeline, enabling them to create custom shaders and achieve unique visual effects.

4. Integration with Web Technologies:

WebGL seamlessly integrates with other web technologies, such as HTML, CSS, and JavaScript, allowing for interactive and dynamic 3D web applications and games.

Setting Up WebGL

To get started with WebGL, you need to create a WebGL context within an HTML5 `<canvas>` element. Here's a simplified example:

```javascript
// Get a reference to the canvas element
const canvas = document.getElementById("myCanvas");

// Get the WebGL context
const gl = canvas.getContext("webgl");
```

```
if (!gl) {
    // WebGL is not supported, handle the error
    alert("WebGL is not available in your browser.");
} else {
    // WebGL is supported, proceed with 3D rendering
    // ...
}
```

In this code, we obtain the WebGL context and check if it's available. If supported, you can proceed with 3D rendering.

Rendering 3D Graphics with WebGL

WebGL relies on shaders, small programs written in GLSL (OpenGL Shading Language), to control the rendering process. Shaders are executed on the GPU and define how vertices and fragments (pixels) are processed to create the final image.

A basic WebGL rendering pipeline involves the following steps:

1. **Vertex Shader:** This shader processes each vertex of 3D objects, transforming them from 3D space to 2D space (screen coordinates).

2. **Fragment Shader:** The fragment shader calculates the color of each pixel (fragment) on the screen. It's responsible for shading, lighting, and texturing effects.

3. **Buffers and Data:** WebGL uses buffers to store and manage data, such as vertex positions, colors, and texture coordinates.

4. **Drawing:** Using the shaders and data, WebGL draws the 3D objects to the canvas.

WebGL Libraries and Frameworks

While working directly with WebGL can be powerful, it can also be complex and time-consuming. Many libraries and frameworks, such as Three.js and Babylon.js, provide abstractions and tools to simplify 3D graphics development in JavaScript games.

Summary

WebGL is a potent technology for adding advanced 3D graphics and visual effects to JavaScript games. Its ability to leverage GPU hardware acceleration, cross-platform compatibility, and integration with web technologies makes it a compelling choice for creating immersive and visually stunning game environments. Whether you're creating complex simulations, interactive experiences, or 3D games, WebGL opens up a world of possibilities for web-based 3D graphics.

4.2. Particle Systems and Special Effects

Particle systems are a vital tool in game development for creating various special effects, such as fire, smoke, explosions, and magical spells. In this section, we'll explore how to implement particle systems in JavaScript games to add dynamic and immersive visual effects.

Understanding Particle Systems

A particle system is a technique used to simulate and render a large number of small, discrete objects (particles) that collectively create dynamic visual effects. Each particle has attributes like position, velocity, size, color, and lifespan. These attributes can change over time, giving rise to various effects.

Particle systems are versatile and can be used for a wide range of effects, including:

- **Fire and Smoke:** Create realistic fire and smoke effects by animating particles with varying colors, sizes, and lifespans.

- **Explosions:** Simulate explosive effects with rapidly expanding and dissipating particles.

- **Water Splashes:** Render water splashes and droplets when objects hit a liquid surface.

- **Magical Spells:** Add mystic and enchanting visuals to spells and magical abilities.

Implementing a Simple Particle System

To implement a basic particle system, follow these steps:

1. **Particle Initialization:** Define the attributes of each particle, including position, velocity, size, color, and lifespan.

2. **Particle Update:** In the game loop, update the particle attributes based on their behavior. For example, particles may move according to their velocity, change color over time, and gradually reduce their lifespan.

3. **Particle Rendering:** Render the particles on the canvas. Use their attributes to determine their appearance, such as size, color, and transparency.

Here's a simplified example of creating a particle system for a fire effect:

```javascript
// Define the particle class
class Particle {
  constructor(x, y) {
    this.x = x;
    this.y = y;
    this.velocityX = Math.random() * 2 - 1; // Random horizontal velocity
    this.velocityY = Math.random() * -3 - 1; // Random upward velocity
    this.size = Math.random() * 5 + 2; // Random size
```

```javascript
    this.color = "rgba(255, " + Math.floor(Math.random() * 100) + ", 0, 0.5)"
; // Random color
    this.lifespan = 100; // Lifespan of the particle
  }

  update() {
    // Update position and size
    this.x += this.velocityX;
    this.y += this.velocityY;
    this.size -= 0.2;
    this.lifespan--;

    // Reset particle if it's too small or expired
    if (this.size <= 0 || this.lifespan <= 0) {
      this.x = mouseX; // Reposition particle at mouse cursor
      this.y = mouseY;
      this.velocityX = Math.random() * 2 - 1;
      this.velocityY = Math.random() * -3 - 1;
      this.size = Math.random() * 5 + 2;
      this.color = "rgba(255, " + Math.floor(Math.random() * 100) + ", 0, 0.5
)";
      this.lifespan = 100;
    }
  }

  render(ctx) {
    // Render the particle as a circle
    ctx.fillStyle = this.color;
    ctx.beginPath();
    ctx.arc(this.x, this.y, this.size, 0, Math.PI * 2);
    ctx.fill();
  }
}

// Create an array to hold particles
const particles = [];

// Game Loop
function gameLoop() {
  // Clear the canvas
  ctx.clearRect(0, 0, canvas.width, canvas.height);

  // Create new particles at mouse cursor
  canvas.addEventListener("mousemove", (event) => {
    mouseX = event.clientX;
    mouseY = event.clientY;
    for (let i = 0; i < 5; i++) {
      particles.push(new Particle(mouseX, mouseY));
    }
```

```
});

// Update and render particles
for (let i = 0; i < particles.length; i++) {
  particles[i].update();
  particles[i].render(ctx);
}

// Remove expired particles
particles = particles.filter((particle) => particle.lifespan > 0);

requestAnimationFrame(gameLoop);
}

// Start the game loop
gameLoop();
```

In this example, particles are created and rendered as circles with random colors, sizes, and lifespans. The particles move upward and gradually fade out as they age. When a particle's size or lifespan reaches a threshold, it's reset at the mouse cursor position, creating a continuous fire effect.

Advanced Particle Systems

While the example above demonstrates a simple particle system, advanced systems can incorporate features like gravity, wind, collision detection, and more complex behaviors to achieve a wide range of visual effects. Libraries and frameworks like Three.js and PIXI.js offer extensive support for particle systems and can streamline their implementation in 3D contexts.

Summary

Particle systems are a valuable tool for adding dynamic and immersive visual effects to JavaScript games. By simulating and rendering numerous particles with varying attributes, you can create effects like fire, smoke, explosions, and magical spells. Understanding particle behavior and incorporating advanced features can elevate your game's visual appeal and immersion.

4.3. Shaders and Advanced Rendering Techniques

Shaders play a pivotal role in advanced graphics rendering in JavaScript games. In this section, we'll delve into shaders and explore how they enable developers to implement sophisticated visual effects and customization in WebGL-based game development.

A shader is a small program that runs on the GPU and determines the color and appearance of each pixel on the screen. Shaders are written in languages like GLSL (OpenGL Shading Language) and are executed for each vertex (vertex shader) or pixel (fragment shader) during rendering.

Vertex Shader:
- Responsible for transforming vertex positions from 3D world coordinates to 2D screen coordinates.

- Used for vertex manipulation, such as translations, rotations, and scaling.

Fragment Shader:
- Computes the color and attributes of each pixel.

- Used for determining pixel color, applying lighting, textures, and other visual effects.

Shaders can create a wide range of effects, from basic coloring to complex simulations of materials, lighting, and atmospheric effects.

Types of Shaders

1. **Vertex Shaders:** These shaders manipulate vertex positions. They are used for transformations and can be used to create effects like vertex displacement for water surfaces or terrain.

2. **Fragment Shaders:** These shaders determine the color and appearance of each pixel. They are crucial for applying textures, lighting, and post-processing effects like blur or bloom.

Implementing Shaders

To use shaders in your JavaScript game, you need to follow these steps:

1. **Compile and Link Shaders:** Write your shader code in GLSL, compile it, and link it into a shader program.

2. **Set Shader Uniforms:** Set uniforms (variables that remain constant during rendering) for your shaders. Uniforms can be used to pass data like matrices, colors, and texture samplers.

3. **Activate Shader Program:** Before rendering objects that use a specific shader, activate the shader program.

4. **Rendering with Shaders:** When rendering objects, the active shader program will be used to determine vertex and fragment processing.

Here's a simplified example of using shaders in WebGL:

```javascript
// Compile and link shaders
const vertexShaderSource = `
  // Vertex shader code
`;

const fragmentShaderSource = `
  // Fragment shader code
`;

const vertexShader = gl.createShader(gl.VERTEX_SHADER);
gl.shaderSource(vertexShader, vertexShaderSource);
gl.compileShader(vertexShader);

const fragmentShader = gl.createShader(gl.FRAGMENT_SHADER);
gl.shaderSource(fragmentShader, fragmentShaderSource);
gl.compileShader(fragmentShader);

const shaderProgram = gl.createProgram();
gl.attachShader(shaderProgram, vertexShader);
gl.attachShader(shaderProgram, fragmentShader);
gl.linkProgram(shaderProgram);
gl.useProgram(shaderProgram);

// Set shader uniforms
const colorUniform = gl.getUniformLocation(shaderProgram, "u_color");
gl.uniform4fv(colorUniform, [1.0, 0.0, 0.0, 1.0]);

// Activate shader program before rendering
gl.useProgram(shaderProgram);

// Rendering with shaders
// ...
```

In this example, we compile and link vertex and fragment shaders into a shader program. We also set a uniform variable (u_color) and activate the shader program before rendering.

Advanced Shader Techniques

Advanced shader techniques include:

- **Lighting Models:** Implementing realistic lighting models like Phong or physically-based rendering (PBR) to achieve lifelike materials and shading.

- **Post-Processing Effects:** Applying post-processing effects like bloom, depth of field, and motion blur to enhance the final image.

- **Shadow Mapping:** Simulating shadows cast by objects and light sources to improve realism.

- **Environment Mapping:** Creating reflective and refractive surfaces using environment maps.

- **Custom Materials:** Developing custom materials and textures for unique visual styles.

- **Advanced Animations:** Using shaders for complex animations and simulations, such as fluid dynamics or cloth simulations.

Shader Libraries and Frameworks

While writing shaders from scratch can be challenging, there are libraries and frameworks like Three.js and Babylon.js that simplify shader usage and provide high-level abstractions for common graphics tasks.

Summary

Shaders are a powerful tool for implementing advanced rendering techniques and visual effects in JavaScript games. Whether it's simulating realistic lighting, creating post-processing effects, or achieving unique visual styles, shaders offer the flexibility and customization needed to elevate the visual quality and immersion of your game. Understanding shader programming and exploring shader libraries can unlock a world of creative possibilities for your game development projects.

4.4. Graphics Optimization Techniques

Graphics optimization is a critical aspect of game development in JavaScript, especially when working with complex visuals and 3D environments. In this section, we'll explore various optimization techniques to ensure smooth performance in your games.

Why Graphics Optimization Matters

Graphics optimization is essential for the following reasons:

1. **Performance:** Optimized graphics improve your game's frame rate and responsiveness, ensuring a smooth gaming experience.

2. **Compatibility:** Optimization helps your game run smoothly on a wide range of devices, including lower-end hardware.

3. **Battery Life:** On mobile devices, efficient graphics reduce power consumption, prolonging battery life.

4. **User Retention:** Players are more likely to enjoy and continue playing games that perform well and have minimal lag.

Graphics Optimization Techniques

1. *Level of Detail (LOD):* Implement LOD techniques to reduce the complexity of 3D models based on their distance from the camera. Distant objects can use lower-polygon versions to save resources.

2. *Culling:* Implement frustum culling and occlusion culling to avoid rendering objects that are not visible or obstructed by others. This reduces unnecessary rendering calculations.

3. *Texture Atlases:* Use texture atlases to pack multiple textures into a single image. This reduces the number of texture switches, improving rendering performance.

4. *Batching:* Combine multiple objects with the same shader and texture into a single draw call. Batching minimizes the overhead of rendering each object separately.

5. *Shader Optimization:* Optimize shaders by removing unnecessary calculations and reducing the complexity of fragment shaders. Simple shaders are more efficient.

6. *GPU Instancing:* Utilize GPU instancing to render multiple instances of the same object with a single draw call. This is especially useful for rendering many identical objects.

7. *Object Pooling:* Implement object pooling to reuse game objects instead of constantly creating and destroying them. This reduces memory allocations and garbage collection overhead.

8. *Texture Compression:* Use texture compression formats (e.g., DXT, ETC, ASTC) to reduce texture memory usage without sacrificing quality.

9. *Mipmapping:* Generate mipmaps for textures to improve rendering quality at different distances and reduce aliasing artifacts.

10. *Dynamic Resolution:* Implement dynamic resolution scaling based on device performance. Lower-end devices can render the game at a lower resolution for better performance.

11. *Render Batching:* Group objects with similar materials and shaders together to minimize state changes during rendering.

12. *GPU Profiling:* Use GPU profiling tools to identify performance bottlenecks in your graphics pipeline and optimize accordingly.

13. *Frame Rate Management:* Implement frame rate management to cap the maximum frame rate, preventing excessive GPU usage on high-end devices.

JavaScript-Specific Optimization

When optimizing graphics in JavaScript games, consider these language-specific techniques:

- **Avoiding Global Variables:** Minimize the use of global variables, as they can negatively impact performance and memory management. Use local variables and proper scoping.

- **Garbage Collection:** Be mindful of object creation and memory allocation, as excessive garbage collection can lead to frame rate drops. Use object pooling and limit unnecessary object creation.

- **Canvas vs. WebGL:** Choose the appropriate rendering technology based on your game's complexity. WebGL offers better performance for 2D and 3D graphics, while the HTML5 `<canvas>` element may suffice for simpler games.

Testing and Profiling

Optimization is an iterative process. Test your game on various devices and use profiling tools to identify performance bottlenecks. Monitor frame rates and memory usage to ensure your game runs smoothly on different platforms.

Summary

Graphics optimization is essential for delivering a smooth and enjoyable gaming experience in JavaScript. By implementing techniques like LOD, culling, batching, and shader optimization, you can significantly improve performance, compatibility, and user retention. JavaScript-specific optimization strategies and careful testing ensure that your game performs well across a wide range of devices and platforms.

4.5. Integrating Graphics Libraries like Three.js

Integrating graphics libraries like Three.js can significantly simplify the development of complex 3D graphics and interactive experiences in JavaScript games. In this section, we'll explore how to incorporate Three.js into your game development workflow.

What is Three.js?

Three.js is a popular JavaScript library that simplifies the creation and rendering of 3D content in web browsers. It abstracts many low-level WebGL operations, making it easier for developers to work with 3D graphics, animations, and interactive elements.

Benefits of Using Three.js

1. **Abstraction of WebGL:** Three.js provides a high-level abstraction over WebGL, reducing the complexity of low-level WebGL code and making 3D graphics more accessible to developers.

2. **Cross-Browser Compatibility:** Three.js ensures compatibility with various web browsers, handling browser-specific WebGL implementations and quirks.

3. **Rich Features:** Three.js offers a wide range of features, including camera controls, lighting, materials, textures, and physics simulations, allowing you to create immersive 3D environments.

4. **Active Community:** Three.js has a thriving community and extensive documentation, making it easier to find solutions to common challenges and receive support.

Getting Started with Three.js

To begin using Three.js in your JavaScript game, follow these basic steps:

1. **Include Three.js:** Download the Three.js library or link to it using a Content Delivery Network (CDN) in your HTML file:

```
<script src="https://cdnjs.cloudflare.com/ajax/libs/three.js/r128/three.min.js"></script>
```

2. **Creating a Scene:** Set up a Three.js scene, camera, and renderer:

```
const scene = new THREE.Scene();
const camera = new THREE.PerspectiveCamera(75, window.innerWidth / window.innerHeight, 0.1, 1000);
const renderer = new THREE.WebGLRenderer();
renderer.setSize(window.innerWidth, window.innerHeight);
document.body.appendChild(renderer.domElement);
```

3. **Adding Objects:** Create 3D objects and add them to the scene:

```
const geometry = new THREE.BoxGeometry();
const material = new THREE.MeshBasicMaterial({ color: 0x00ff00 });
const cube = new THREE.Mesh(geometry, material);
scene.add(cube);
```

4. **Animating:** Implement animation by updating the object's properties in the animation loop:

```
const animate = () => {
  requestAnimationFrame(animate);

  cube.rotation.x += 0.01;
  cube.rotation.y += 0.01;

  renderer.render(scene, camera);
};

animate();
```

Advanced Features in Three.js

Three.js offers numerous advanced features for creating complex 3D games:

- **Camera Controls:** Implement camera controls for user interaction, including orbit controls and first-person camera movements.

- **Lights and Shadows:** Utilize different types of lights (ambient, directional, point, spot) and shadows to enhance realism.

- **Materials and Textures:** Apply materials, textures, and shaders to objects to achieve realistic surfaces and visual effects.

- **Physics Simulations:** Use libraries like Cannon.js or Ammo.js to implement physics simulations for realistic object interactions and dynamics.

- **Importing 3D Models:** Import external 3D models created in software like Blender or Maya into your Three.js scene.

- **Particle Systems:** Create particle systems for effects like fire, smoke, and explosions.

- **Post-Processing:** Apply post-processing effects like bloom, motion blur, and depth of field for enhanced visuals.

Examples and Resources

To further your knowledge of Three.js, explore official documentation, tutorials, and examples available on the official Three.js website and community-driven resources. The Three.js community is active and supportive, making it a valuable asset in your journey to creating impressive 3D games with JavaScript.

Summary

Integrating graphics libraries like Three.js into your JavaScript game development process can streamline the creation of complex 3D graphics and interactive experiences. With its abstraction of WebGL, rich features, cross-browser compatibility, and strong community, Three.js offers a powerful toolset for building immersive and visually stunning 3D games for the web.

Chapter 5: Sound and Music Integration

5.1. Basics of Web Audio API

The integration of sound and music is a crucial element in game development, enhancing the overall gaming experience. In this section, we'll explore the basics of the Web Audio API in JavaScript, which allows you to work with audio in web-based games.

The Web Audio API is a JavaScript API designed for handling audio operations in web applications, including games. It provides a powerful and flexible way to create, manipulate, and play audio in real-time. Some of the key features of the Web Audio API include:

- **Audio Context:** The central hub for audio processing, where you can create audio sources, effects, and manipulate audio data.

- **Audio Sources:** Represent sound sources, such as audio files or generated audio data. These sources can be played, paused, and controlled.

- **Audio Effects:** Apply various audio effects like reverb, equalization, and panning to audio sources to enhance the audio experience.

- **Real-time Audio Manipulation:** Modify audio data in real-time, allowing for dynamic sound effects based on game events.

Creating an Audio Context

To get started with the Web Audio API, you need to create an Audio Context:

```
const audioContext = new (window.AudioContext || window.webkitAudioContext)();
```

The code above creates an Audio Context, which serves as the foundation for all audio operations in your game.

Loading and Playing Audio

You can load and play audio files using the Web Audio API. Here's an example of loading and playing an audio file:

```
// Create an audio element
const audioElement = new Audio('background_music.mp3');

// Create an audio source from the element
const audioSource = audioContext.createMediaElementSource(audioElement);

// Connect the source to the audio context's output (speakers)
audioSource.connect(audioContext.destination);

// Play the audio
audioElement.play();
```

In this example, we create an `Audio` element, convert it to an audio source using `createMediaElementSource`, and connect it to the audio context's output to play the audio.

Besides playing audio files, you can also generate audio data dynamically using the Web Audio API. For example, you can create oscillators to generate tones:

```
// Create an oscillator
const oscillator = audioContext.createOscillator();

// Set the frequency (440 Hz for A4)
oscillator.frequency.setValueAtTime(440, audioContext.currentTime);

// Connect the oscillator to the audio context's output
oscillator.connect(audioContext.destination);

// Start and stop the oscillator
oscillator.start();
oscillator.stop(audioContext.currentTime + 1); // Stop after 1 second
```

In this code, we create an oscillator, set its frequency, connect it to the audio context's output, and start and stop it to generate a tone.

Summary

The Web Audio API is a powerful tool for integrating sound and music into your JavaScript games. It allows you to load and play audio files, generate audio data dynamically, and apply various audio effects to enhance the gaming experience. Understanding the basics of the Web Audio API is essential for creating immersive and engaging audio in your games.

5.2. Adding Background Music and Sound Effects

Incorporating background music and sound effects is a vital part of creating an immersive gaming experience. In this section, we'll explore how to add background music and sound effects to your JavaScript games using the Web Audio API.

Background Music

Background music sets the tone for your game and can significantly enhance the atmosphere. To add background music, follow these steps:

1. **Load the Audio File:**

   – Load your background music audio file, typically in MP3 or OGG format, into your game's assets.

2. **Create an Audio Source:**

   – Use the Web Audio API to create an audio source from the loaded file.

3. **Connect to the Audio Context:**

   - Connect the audio source to the Audio Context's destination (speakers) to ensure the music is audible.

4. **Control Playback:**

   - Implement play, pause, and volume controls for the background music to allow users to customize their audio experience.

Here's a simplified example of adding background music to your game:

```
const audioContext = new (window.AudioContext || window.webkitAudioContext)();
const backgroundMusic = new Audio('background_music.mp3');
const backgroundMusicSource = audioContext.createMediaElementSource(backgroundMusic);

// Connect the background music source to the audio context's output
backgroundMusicSource.connect(audioContext.destination);

// Play the background music
backgroundMusic.play();
```

This code creates an Audio Context, loads the background music, and connects it to the audio context for playback.

Sound Effects

Sound effects provide auditory feedback for in-game actions and events. To add sound effects, follow these steps:

1. **Load Sound Effect Files:**

   - Load your sound effect audio files (e.g., gunfire, explosions, footsteps) into your game's assets.

2. **Create Audio Sources:**

   - For each sound effect, create an audio source using the Web Audio API.

3. **Connect to the Audio Context:**

   - Connect each sound effect source to the Audio Context's destination.

4. **Trigger Sound Effects:**

   - Implement event listeners or functions that trigger specific sound effects based on in-game events.

Here's a simplified example of adding a sound effect to your game:

```
const audioContext = new (window.AudioContext || window.webkitAudioContext)();
```

```
const gunshotSound = new Audio('gunshot.mp3');
const gunshotSoundSource = audioContext.createMediaElementSource(gunshotSound
);

// Connect the gunshot sound source to the audio context's output
gunshotSoundSource.connect(audioContext.destination);

// Trigger the gunshot sound on a game event
function playGunshotSound() {
  gunshotSound.play();
}

// Example: Call playGunshotSound() when a player shoots in the game
```

In this code, we create an Audio Context, load a gunshot sound effect, and trigger it when a player shoots in the game.

Audio Optimization and Best Practices

To ensure a smooth audio experience in your game, consider these optimization and best practices:

- **Audio Preloading:** Preload audio assets to reduce delays when playing sounds.

- **Audio Compression:** Use compressed audio formats (e.g., MP3, OGG) to minimize file size while maintaining quality.

- **Volume Control:** Allow users to adjust the volume of background music and sound effects separately.

- **Audio Panning:** Implement stereo panning to create a sense of direction for sound effects.

- **Memory Management:** Be mindful of memory usage when loading and unloading audio assets to avoid memory leaks.

- **Audio Sprite Sheets:** Use audio sprite sheets to combine multiple sound effects into a single audio file for efficient loading and playback.

- **Cross-Browser Compatibility:** Test audio playback across different web browsers to ensure compatibility.

- **Audio Pooling:** Implement sound effect pooling to reuse and manage sound effect instances efficiently.

- **Fallback Mechanisms:** Provide fallbacks for audio playback in case the Web Audio API is not supported in some browsers.

Summary

Adding background music and sound effects to your JavaScript games using the Web Audio API can significantly enhance the gaming experience. By following best practices, optimizing audio assets, and providing user control over audio settings, you can create immersive and engaging audio experiences that complement your game's visuals and gameplay.

5.3. Controlling Audio Playback and Volume

Controlling audio playback and volume is essential for creating a polished gaming experience. In this section, we'll explore how to manage audio playback and adjust audio volume in your JavaScript games using the Web Audio API.

Playback Control

Controlling audio playback involves managing when audio starts, stops, pauses, resumes, and loops. Here are some common scenarios:

Playing Background Music

To play background music, you typically load the audio file and start playback. You can use the play() method of the audio element:

```
const backgroundMusic = new Audio('background_music.mp3');
backgroundMusic.play();
```

Pausing and Resuming

You can pause and resume audio playback using the pause() and play() methods:

```
// Pause background music
backgroundMusic.pause();

// Resume background music
backgroundMusic.play();
```

Stopping

To stop audio playback and reset it to the beginning, you can use the pause() method followed by setting the currentTime property to 0:

```
// Stop background music
backgroundMusic.pause();
backgroundMusic.currentTime = 0;
```

Looping

To create a continuous loop of background music, set the `loop` property to `true`:

```
backgroundMusic.loop = true;
```

Volume Control

Adjusting audio volume is crucial for allowing players to customize their gaming experience. The Web Audio API provides a `GainNode` that allows you to control audio volume programmatically.

Creating a GainNode

To control volume, create a `GainNode` and connect it between the audio source and the destination:

```
const audioContext = new (window.AudioContext || window.webkitAudioContext)();
const audioSource = audioContext.createMediaElementSource(backgroundMusic);
const gainNode = audioContext.createGain();

// Connect the audio source to the gain node
audioSource.connect(gainNode);

// Connect the gain node to the audio context's output
gainNode.connect(audioContext.destination);
```

Adjusting Volume

You can adjust the volume using the gainNode's gain property, which ranges from 0 (silent) to 1 (full volume). For example, to set the volume to 50%:

```
gainNode.gain.value = 0.5;
```

Volume Control UI

To allow users to control volume through a UI element, you can create sliders or buttons that update the gain value when adjusted:

```
const volumeSlider = document.getElementById('volume-slider');

// Update volume when the slider is adjusted
volumeSlider.addEventListener('input', () => {
  const volumeValue = parseFloat(volumeSlider.value);
  gainNode.gain.value = volumeValue;
});
```

In this example, the volume slider's input event updates the gain value based on the slider's position.

Summary

Controlling audio playback and volume in your JavaScript games using the Web Audio API is essential for creating an engaging and user-friendly experience. By managing when audio starts, stops, pauses, and resumes, as well as providing volume control options, you can tailor the audio experience to suit your players' preferences. These features contribute to the overall immersion and enjoyment of your game.

5.4. Interactive Audio: Responding to Game Events

Interactive audio that responds to in-game events adds depth and immersion to your JavaScript games. In this section, we'll explore how to trigger and synchronize audio effects with game events using the Web Audio API.

Event-Driven Audio

Event-driven audio allows you to play sound effects, voice lines, or music in response to specific in-game events. These events can include player actions, character interactions, environmental changes, and more. Here's how to implement event-driven audio:

1. **Define Game Events:** Identify the events in your game that should trigger audio responses. For example, a "coin collected" event or a "player hit" event.

2. **Load Audio Assets:** Prepare the audio files or samples associated with each event.

3. **Create Audio Sources:** Use the Web Audio API to create audio sources for each audio asset.

4. **Event Listeners:** Implement event listeners or callbacks that trigger the audio playback when the corresponding in-game events occur.

5. **Control Playback:** Adjust the playback settings, such as volume, pitch, and spatial positioning, to match the context of the game event.

Example: Coin Collection Sound

Let's consider an example of triggering a sound effect when a player collects a coin in a game. Here's how you can implement this using the Web Audio API:

```
const audioContext = new (window.AudioContext || window.webkitAudioContext)();
const coinCollectSound = new Audio('coin_collect.mp3');
const coinCollectSoundSource = audioContext.createMediaElementSource(coinCollectSound);

// Connect the coin collection sound source to the audio context's output
coinCollectSoundSource.connect(audioContext.destination);
```

```
// Function to play the coin collection sound
function playCoinCollectSound() {
  coinCollectSound.currentTime = 0; // Rewind to the beginning
  coinCollectSound.play();
}

// Example: Trigger the coin collection sound when a player collects a coin
function onCoinCollected() {
  // Handle coin collection logic
  playCoinCollectSound(); // Play the sound effect
}
```

In this example, we create an event listener (onCoinCollected) that plays the coin collection sound when a player collects a coin. The sound is rewound to the beginning each time it's played to allow rapid consecutive plays.

Spatial Audio

For more immersive experiences, consider implementing spatial audio, which simulates the direction and distance of sounds in the game world. Spatial audio adds realism and can help players locate objects or events by sound.

To implement spatial audio, you can use the Web Audio API's spatialization features. These features allow you to position audio sources in 3D space and control how they interact with the player's perspective.

Audio Synchronization

In some cases, audio events may need to be synchronized precisely with game events or animations. To achieve this synchronization, you can use the Web Audio API's scheduling features. You can schedule audio playback to start at specific times or in synchronization with other game elements.

Summary

Implementing interactive audio that responds to in-game events enhances the player's experience and immersion in your JavaScript games. By identifying the events, loading audio assets, creating audio sources, and triggering playback in response to game events, you can create a dynamic and engaging audio experience. Additionally, consider spatial audio and audio synchronization to further elevate the audio quality of your games.

5.5. Audio Optimization and Best Practices

Optimizing audio in your JavaScript games is essential to ensure smooth gameplay and a great user experience. In this section, we'll explore various audio optimization techniques and best practices to follow when working with the Web Audio API.

1. Audio Asset Format

Choosing the right audio asset format is crucial for optimization. Common formats like MP3 and OGG offer a good balance between audio quality and file size. Consider the following:

- Use MP3 or OGG for music and sound effects.
- Compress audio assets to reduce file size while maintaining acceptable quality.
- Test audio compatibility across different web browsers.

2. Audio Preloading

Preloading audio assets before they are needed ensures that they are readily available during gameplay, reducing delays when triggering sound effects or background music. You can preload audio assets using JavaScript to improve performance.

```
const audio = new Audio('background_music.mp3');
audio.preload = 'auto';
```

3. Audio Sprite Sheets

Audio sprite sheets combine multiple sound effects into a single audio file. This technique reduces the number of HTTP requests for audio assets and improves loading times.

You can use libraries like Howler.js to work with audio sprite sheets efficiently.

```
const spriteSheet = new Howl({
  src: ['audio_sprite_sheet.mp3'],
  sprite: {
    gunshot: [0, 1000],
    explosion: [2000, 1500],
    powerup: [4000, 800],
  },
});
```

4. Memory Management

Managing memory when loading and unloading audio assets is crucial to prevent memory leaks. When audio assets are no longer needed, release them properly.

```
const audio = new Audio('sound_effect.mp3');

// When the sound effect is no longer needed, release it
audio.src = '';
audio.load();
audio = null;
```

5. Volume Control

Allow users to adjust the volume of background music and sound effects separately. Implement volume sliders or settings to give players control over their audio experience.

```
const audioContext = new (window.AudioContext || window.webkitAudioContext)();
const gainNode = audioContext.createGain();

// Adjust the volume using gainNode.gain.value
```

6. Audio Panning

Implement stereo panning to create a sense of direction for sound effects. This can enhance the player's perception of the game world.

```
const panNode = audioContext.createStereoPanner();
panNode.pan.value = -1; // Fully left
```

7. Cross-Browser Compatibility

Test audio playback across different web browsers to ensure compatibility. Some browsers may have limitations or differences in audio support, so it's essential to check and provide fallback mechanisms if needed.

8. Audio Pooling

Implement audio pooling for frequently used sound effects. Instead of creating a new audio source for each play, you can reuse existing sources, reducing the overhead of audio source creation.

```
const audioPool = [];
const maxPoolSize = 10;

function playSoundEffect(src) {
  let audio;
  if (audioPool.length < maxPoolSize) {
    audio = new Audio(src);
    audioPool.push(audio);
  } else {
    audio = audioPool.shift();
    audio.src = src;
  }
  audio.play();
}
```

9. Fallback Mechanisms

Provide fallback mechanisms for audio playback in case the Web Audio API is not supported in some browsers. You can use the <audio> element as a fallback or consider other audio libraries that offer broader compatibility.

10. Performance Testing

Regularly test and profile your game's audio performance to identify and address any bottlenecks. Tools like the Chrome DevTools can help you monitor audio-related metrics and optimize accordingly.

By following these audio optimization techniques and best practices, you can ensure that audio in your JavaScript games contributes positively to the overall gaming experience while maintaining optimal performance.

Chapter 6: Building Game Worlds

6.1. Designing Game Levels and Worlds

Designing game levels and worlds is a crucial aspect of game development that directly impacts the player's experience. Whether you are creating a platformer, an RPG, or a puzzle game, thoughtful level and world design can make your game more engaging and enjoyable. In this section, we will explore the key principles and techniques for designing game levels and worlds in JavaScript gaming.

1. Concept and Theme

Start by defining the concept and theme of your game. What is the story or objective? What kind of world will your players explore? Establishing a clear vision for your game world will guide your level design.

2. Paper Prototyping

Before diving into digital level design, consider using paper prototypes. Sketch out your level layouts and gameplay mechanics on paper to visualize how they will work. This low-tech approach allows for quick iterations and adjustments.

3. Flow and Pacing

Maintain a balance between challenging and relaxing moments in your levels. Design the flow to provide players with a sense of accomplishment while keeping them engaged. Use pacing to control the rhythm of your game, introducing new challenges gradually.

4. Player Progression

Design levels with a sense of progression. Start with easier challenges to help players learn the game mechanics and gradually increase the difficulty. Provide rewards or power-ups as players advance.

5. Playtesting

Regular playtesting is essential. Invite testers to play your levels and gather feedback. Pay attention to how players navigate your levels and adjust them based on their experiences.

6. Environmental Storytelling

Use level design to tell a story. Environmental storytelling involves conveying narrative elements through the game world itself. Place objects, signs, or visual cues that hint at the game's backstory or upcoming challenges.

7. Non-Linear Paths

Consider adding branching paths or non-linear progression in your levels. This encourages exploration and replayability. Players can choose different routes, uncover secrets, or make choices that affect the story.

8. Balancing Challenges

Balance the difficulty of your levels. Gradually introduce new mechanics and challenges, ensuring that they are fair and not overly frustrating. Use playtesting to fine-tune the difficulty.

9. Aesthetics and Atmosphere

Pay attention to the visual and audio elements that contribute to the atmosphere of your levels. Art, music, and sound effects should align with the theme and create a cohesive experience.

10. Accessibility

Consider accessibility in level design. Ensure that your levels can be enjoyed by players with different abilities. Provide options for adjustable difficulty or alternative paths for challenging sections.

11. Iteration

Level design is an iterative process. Don't be afraid to revisit and refine your levels multiple times. Feedback from playtesting and observing player behavior can lead to significant improvements.

12. Documentation

Document your level designs, including layouts, mechanics, and any special events or triggers. Clear documentation helps your team understand and implement your vision effectively.

Remember that level and world design is a creative process, and there are no one-size-fits-all solutions. Experiment, gather feedback, and iterate to create levels that captivate players and enhance their gaming experience.

6.2. Tilemaps and Background Scrolling

Tilemaps and background scrolling are fundamental techniques in game development, especially for 2D games. They allow you to efficiently create large game worlds and provide a seamless gaming experience. In this section, we will explore how to implement tilemaps and background scrolling in JavaScript games.

1. Tilemaps

Tilemaps are a grid-based system where each cell represents a specific portion of your game world. These cells, known as tiles, can be used to construct the terrain, objects, and environments of your game. Tilemaps are particularly useful for games with grid-based movement, such as platformers and top-down RPGs.

To implement tilemaps in JavaScript, you can create a 2D array where each element corresponds to a specific tile type or terrain feature. For example, you might use the number 0 to represent empty space, 1 for solid ground, and so on. By iterating through this array and rendering the appropriate tiles at the corresponding positions, you can build your game world.

2. Tiled Editors

Tiled is a popular open-source map editor that facilitates the creation of tilemaps for games. It allows you to design levels visually and export them in various formats, including JSON or XML, which can be easily loaded into your game using JavaScript. Integrating Tiled into your workflow can streamline the level design process.

Here's a basic example of loading a tilemap in JavaScript using the Tiled format and rendering it onto a canvas:

```javascript
// Load the tilemap data (assuming 'map.json' is your Tiled export)
fetch('map.json')
  .then(response => response.json())
  .then(data => {
    // Iterate through the tilemap data and render tiles
    data.layers.forEach(layer => {
      if (layer.type === 'tilelayer') {
        layer.data.forEach((tile, index) => {
          // Render 'tile' at 'index' position
          // You'll need to map 'tile' to your tileset graphics
          // based on the tileset used in Tiled.
        });
      }
    });
  });
```

3. Background Scrolling

Background scrolling is essential for games that feature large, continuous game worlds, such as endless runners or shooters. It creates the illusion of movement while keeping the player character centered on the screen.

To implement background scrolling, you can use two or more background layers. As the player character moves, you scroll the background layers at different speeds to create a parallax effect. The foreground elements, including the player character and interactive objects, remain stationary on top of the scrolling background.

Here's a simplified example of horizontal background scrolling in JavaScript:

```javascript
// Initialize background layers
const background1 = new Image();
background1.src = 'background1.png';

const background2 = new Image();
background2.src = 'background2.png';

// Define scrolling speeds
const scrollSpeed1 = 1; // Slower background
const scrollSpeed2 = 2; // Faster background

// Update function in your game loop
function update() {
  // Scroll backgrounds
  background1.x -= scrollSpeed1;
  background2.x -= scrollSpeed2;

  // Reset backgrounds when they move off-screen
  if (background1.x < -background1.width) {
    background1.x = canvas.width;
  }
  if (background2.x < -background2.width) {
    background2.x = canvas.width;
  }

  // Update other game elements here
}

// Render function in your game loop
function render() {
  // Clear the canvas
  context.clearRect(0, 0, canvas.width, canvas.height);

  // Draw backgrounds at their positions
  context.drawImage(background1, background1.x, 0);
  context.drawImage(background2, background2.x, 0);

  // Render other game elements here
}
```

This code demonstrates a simple parallax scrolling effect with two background layers, each scrolling at a different speed. You can expand upon this concept for more complex scrolling scenarios or vertical scrolling.

Incorporating tilemaps and background scrolling into your game design can significantly enhance the visual and interactive aspects of your game world, providing players with a more immersive experience.

6.3. Procedural Generation Techniques

Procedural generation is a powerful approach used in game development to create game worlds, levels, or content algorithmically rather than designing them manually. It enables developers to generate vast and diverse game environments dynamically, providing players with unique experiences. In this section, we will explore procedural generation techniques in JavaScript game development.

1. Randomization

One of the simplest forms of procedural generation is randomization. By using random numbers, you can generate various game elements such as terrain features, enemy placements, item locations, and more. JavaScript's Math.random() function is commonly used for this purpose.

```javascript
// Generate a random number between min (inclusive) and max (exclusive)
function getRandom(min, max) {
    return Math.floor(Math.random() * (max - min)) + min;
}
```

```javascript
// Example usage: Randomize enemy positions
const enemies = [];
for (let i = 0; i < 10; i++) {
    const enemyX = getRandom(0, canvasWidth);
    const enemyY = getRandom(0, canvasHeight);
    enemies.push({ x: enemyX, y: enemyY });
}
```

2. Perlin Noise

Perlin noise is a popular technique for creating natural-looking procedural content, such as terrain and landscapes. In JavaScript, libraries like the noisejs library can be used to generate Perlin noise. You can adjust parameters to control the smoothness and detail of the generated noise.

```javascript
// Example using noisejs to generate 2D Perlin noise
const noise = new Noise(Math.random());

const gridSize = 50;
const noiseScale = 0.1;

const terrain = [];
for (let x = 0; x < canvasWidth; x += gridSize) {
    for (let y = 0; y < canvasHeight; y += gridSize) {
        const value = noise.perlin2(x * noiseScale, y * noiseScale);
        terrain.push({ x, y, value });
```

```
    }
}
```

3. Cellular Automata

Cellular automata are used for generating patterns and structures, such as caves, dungeons, or mazes. The technique involves defining rules for how cells evolve over iterations. Each cell's state depends on its neighbors, leading to emergent patterns.

```
// Example of cellular automata for generating a cave-like map
function initializeMap(width, height) {
  const map = [];
  for (let x = 0; x < width; x++) {
    const column = [];
    for (let y = 0; y < height; y++) {
      // Initialize cells randomly (e.g., 40% chance of being 'alive')
      const isAlive = Math.random() < 0.4;
      column.push(isAlive);
    }
    map.push(column);
  }
  return map;
}

function iterateMap(map) {
  // Implement cellular automata rules for map evolution here
  // Typically, you'd define rules for cell birth, death, and survival
  // based on the state of neighboring cells.
}

// Initialize and iterate the map for cave generation
const caveMap = initializeMap(canvasWidth, canvasHeight);
for (let i = 0; i < numIterations; i++) {
  caveMap = iterateMap(caveMap);
}
```

4. L-Systems

Lindenmayer systems (L-systems) are used to generate complex shapes and structures, such as plants, trees, and fractals. They consist of a set of rules that iteratively replace symbols in a string to create the final pattern.

```
// Example of an L-system for generating a fractal tree
const axiom = 'F';
const rules = {
  'F': 'FF+[+F-F-F]-[-F+F+F]'
};

function applyRules(sentence) {
  let newSentence = '';
```

```
  for (let i = 0; i < sentence.length; i++) {
    const current = sentence[i];
    if (rules[current]) {
      newSentence += rules[current];
    } else {
      newSentence += current;
    }
  }
  return newSentence;
}

// Generate the fractal tree by applying rules iteratively
let sentence = axiom;
for (let i = 0; i < numIterations; i++) {
  sentence = applyRules(sentence);
}
```

Procedural generation techniques provide a means to create diverse and dynamic game content, enhancing replayability and expanding the possibilities for game design in JavaScript. Depending on your game's requirements, you can combine these techniques or explore other methods to achieve the desired procedural content generation.

6.4. Implementing Physics and Gravity

Implementing physics and gravity is crucial for creating realistic and engaging game worlds in JavaScript game development. Physics engines and gravity simulation are used to handle object movement, collisions, and interactions. In this section, we will explore how to implement physics and gravity in your JavaScript games.

1. Physics Engines

Physics engines are libraries or frameworks that provide predefined functions and algorithms for simulating real-world physics in games. Some popular JavaScript physics engines include Matter.js, p2.js, and Cannon.js. These engines simplify complex tasks like collision detection, rigid body dynamics, and constraint solving.

Here's a basic example using Matter.js to create a falling box affected by gravity:

```
// Create an engine
const engine = Matter.Engine.create();

// Create a box
const box = Matter.Bodies.rectangle(400, 0, 80, 80);

// Add the box to the world
Matter.World.add(engine.world, [box]);
```

```javascript
// Apply gravity
engine.world.gravity.y = 1; // Adjust gravity strength as needed

// Render the scene
Matter.Render.run(Matter.Render.create({
  element: document.body,
  engine: engine
}));

// Start the engine
Matter.Engine.run(engine);
```

2. Gravity Simulation

Gravity is a fundamental force in many games, affecting the movement of objects and characters. In JavaScript, you can implement gravity by applying a constant force vector (usually in the vertical direction) to objects within your game.

```javascript
// Apply gravity to a game object
const gravity = 0.5; // Adjust gravity strength as needed

function applyGravity(object) {
  object.velocityY += gravity;
}

// In your game loop
function gameLoop() {
  // Update object positions
  applyGravity(player);

  // Check for collisions and resolve them
  // ...

  // Render the scene
  // ...

  requestAnimationFrame(gameLoop);
}
```

In this example, the `applyGravity` function is called in your game loop to update the vertical velocity of the game object, simulating gravity.

3. Collision Detection

Proper collision detection is essential for handling object interactions in your game. Whether you're using a physics engine or implementing collision detection manually, you need to check for collisions between objects and respond accordingly.

Here's a simplified example of manual collision detection between two rectangles:

```javascript
function detectCollision(rect1, rect2) {
  return (
    rect1.x < rect2.x + rect2.width &&
    rect1.x + rect1.width > rect2.x &&
    rect1.y < rect2.y + rect2.height &&
    rect1.y + rect1.height > rect2.y
  );
}

// In your game loop
function gameLoop() {
  // Check for collisions between player and obstacles
  if (detectCollision(player, obstacle)) {
    // Handle the collision (e.g., stop player movement or decrease health)
  }

  // Update object positions
  // ...

  // Render the scene
  // ...

  requestAnimationFrame(gameLoop);
}
```

This code snippet demonstrates a simple collision detection function that checks if two rectangles overlap. You can expand on this concept for more complex collision scenarios.

Implementing physics and gravity in your JavaScript games enhances realism and interactivity, allowing objects to move, interact, and respond to forces like gravity. Depending on the complexity of your game, you may choose to use a physics engine or implement physics logic manually to achieve the desired gameplay experience.

6.5. Environmental Effects and Dynamics

Environmental effects and dynamics play a significant role in creating immersive and engaging game worlds. These elements add realism, depth, and interactivity to the game environment, making it more captivating for players. In this section, we will explore various techniques to implement environmental effects and dynamics in JavaScript game development.

1. Weather and Climate

Weather effects, such as rain, snow, and fog, can enhance the atmosphere of your game. Implementing these effects involves simulating the behavior of particles or objects in the game world. You can use techniques like particle systems to create realistic raindrops or snowflakes falling from the sky.

```javascript
// Example of a simple rain particle system
const raindrops = [];

function createRaindrop() {
  const x = Math.random() * canvasWidth;
  const y = -10; // Start above the canvas
  const speed = Math.random() * 5 + 2; // Random speed
  const length = Math.random() * 10 + 5; // Random length
  raindrops.push({ x, y, speed, length });
}

function updateRaindrops() {
  for (let i = 0; i < raindrops.length; i++) {
    const raindrop = raindrops[i];
    raindrop.y += raindrop.speed;
    // Remove raindrops that fall below the canvas
    if (raindrop.y > canvasHeight) {
      raindrops.splice(i, 1);
      i--;
    }
  }
}

// In your game loop
function gameLoop() {
  createRaindrop();
  updateRaindrops();

  // Render the scene with raindrops
  // ...

  requestAnimationFrame(gameLoop);
}
```

2. Day-Night Cycle

Implementing a day-night cycle can add realism and variation to your game environment. You can control lighting, visibility, and other game elements based on the time of day. JavaScript's Date object or a custom timer can be used to manage the day-night cycle.

```javascript
// Example of a simple day-night cycle
let isDay = true;

function updateDayNightCycle() {
  // Check the current time or timer value to determine day or night
  isDay = /* Check time or timer value */;
```

```
  // Adjust lighting and environmental elements accordingly
  if (isDay) {
    // Apply daytime lighting and effects
    // ...
  } else {
    // Apply nighttime lighting and effects
    // ...
  }
}

// In your game loop
function gameLoop() {
  updateDayNightCycle();

  // Render the scene with appropriate lighting and effects
  // ...

  requestAnimationFrame(gameLoop);
}
```

3. Dynamic Terrain and Ecosystems

For open-world games, dynamic terrain and ecosystems can provide a rich and evolving game environment. You can use procedural generation to create changing landscapes, including terrain features, vegetation, and wildlife. Environmental factors like seasons and weather can influence the game's ecosystem.

```
// Example of dynamic terrain generation based on seasons
const seasons = ['Spring', 'Summer', 'Autumn', 'Winter'];
let currentSeason = 0;

function updateSeason() {
  // Determine the current season based on in-game time or other factors
  currentSeason = /* Determine current season */;

  // Adjust terrain, vegetation, and wildlife based on the season
  if (currentSeason === 'Spring') {
    // Generate lush vegetation and wildlife
    // ...
  } else if (currentSeason === 'Winter') {
    // Create snowy landscapes and adapt wildlife behavior
    // ...
  }
}

// In your game loop
function gameLoop() {
  updateSeason();
```

```
// Render the scene with season-specific terrain and ecosystems
// ...

    requestAnimationFrame(gameLoop);
}
```

Implementing environmental effects and dynamics requires careful consideration of how these elements impact gameplay and the overall experience. By incorporating weather, day-night cycles, and dynamic ecosystems, you can create a more immersive and interactive game world in JavaScript.

7.1. Designing Player Characters

Designing player characters is a fundamental aspect of game development that significantly influences the player's experience. The player character is often the protagonist, and their design affects gameplay, story, and immersion. In this section, we will explore important considerations for designing player characters in JavaScript game development.

Characteristics of a Well-Designed Player Character

A well-designed player character enhances the overall gaming experience. Here are some key characteristics to consider:

1. **Visual Appeal:** The player character's appearance should be visually appealing and consistent with the game's art style. It should be distinct and memorable.

2. **Personality:** Consider the character's personality traits, backstory, and motivations. A well-developed character can create a deeper emotional connection with the player.

3. **Role and Abilities:** Define the character's role in the game world and their unique abilities or skills. These abilities should align with the gameplay mechanics and challenges.

4. **Customization:** If the game allows character customization, provide a range of options for players to personalize their character's appearance and sometimes abilities.

5. **Progression:** Plan character progression throughout the game. Characters may evolve, gain new skills, or face moral dilemmas that impact the storyline.

Player Character Creation Process

Creating a player character involves several steps:

1. Conceptualization

Start by brainstorming and sketching ideas for the character. Consider their role in the game, appearance, personality traits, and how they fit into the game's narrative.

2. Art and Design

Collaborate with artists and designers to create concept art and character designs. Ensure that the character's visual design aligns with the game's overall aesthetic.

3. Animation

Animate the character to bring them to life. Define animations for various actions, such as walking, running, jumping, and interacting with objects.

```javascript
// Example: Creating a player character animation in JavaScript
const playerCharacter = {
  x: 0,
  y: 0,
  spriteSheet: /* Load sprite sheet image */,
  currentFrame: 0,
  frameWidth: 64,
  frameHeight: 64,
  frameCount: 8,
  frameRate: 10, // Frames per second

  // Update function to animate the character
  update: function () {
    this.currentFrame = (this.currentFrame + 1) % this.frameCount;
  },

  // Draw function to render the character
  draw: function () {
    const frameX = this.currentFrame * this.frameWidth;
    // Draw the current frame on the canvas
    // ...
  },
};

// In your game loop
function gameLoop() {
  playerCharacter.update();
  // Other game logic and rendering
}
```

4. Integration

Integrate the character into the game engine, including their movement, interactions, and responses to player input.

5. Testing and Iteration

Test the character in various game scenarios to ensure they function as intended. Gather player feedback and iterate on the character's design and mechanics as needed.

6. Story and Dialogues

If the character has a role in the game's story, write dialogues and narrative elements that reflect their personality and motivations. Dialogue trees and choices can make interactions more engaging.

A well-designed player character contributes to player engagement, immersion, and enjoyment. Whether your game features a heroic adventurer, a quirky protagonist, or a blank slate for player customization, careful design and execution of the player character can elevate your game's experience.

7.2. Implementing Movement and Controls

Implementing movement and controls for the player character is a critical aspect of game development, as it directly impacts how players interact with the game world. In this section, we'll explore various techniques and considerations for implementing character movement and controls in JavaScript games.

Player Movement Basics

Player movement typically involves actions like walking, running, jumping, and crouching. The implementation of character movement can vary depending on the game's genre and mechanics. Here are some common approaches:

1. **Keyboard Input:** Utilize keyboard input to control character movement. Listen for key presses and releases to move the character in the desired direction.

   ```
   // Example: Handling keyboard input for character movement
   document.addEventListener('keydown', (event) => {
     if (event.key === 'ArrowRight') {
       // Move character right
     } else if (event.key === 'ArrowLeft') {
       // Move character left
     }
     // Handle other movement keys
   });
   ```

2. **Gamepad Support:** If your game supports gamepads or controllers, implement support for analog sticks, buttons, and triggers to control character movement.

   ```
   // Example: Handling gamepad input for character movement
   const gamepad = navigator.getGamepads()[0]; // Get the first connected gamepad
   if (gamepad) {
     const leftStickX = gamepad.axes[0]; // X-axis of the left analog stick
     const leftStickY = gamepad.axes[1]; // Y-axis of the left analog stick

     // Use leftStickX and leftStickY to control character movement
   }
   ```

3. **Touch Controls:** For mobile and touch-enabled devices, implement touch controls that allow players to swipe or tap to move the character.

   ```
   // Example: Handling touch controls for character movement
   const touchArea = document.getElementById('touchArea'); // Replace with
   ```

your touch area element

```javascript
touchArea.addEventListener('touchstart', (event) => {
  // Handle touch start event
});

touchArea.addEventListener('touchmove', (event) => {
  // Handle touch move event
});

touchArea.addEventListener('touchend', (event) => {
  // Handle touch end event
});
```

Physics and Collision Detection

Incorporating physics and collision detection is crucial to ensure that the player character interacts realistically with the game world. Implement collision checks to prevent the character from passing through walls or obstacles.

```javascript
// Example: Simple collision detection for character and obstacles
function checkCollision(character, obstacle) {
  // Check if character's bounding box overlaps with obstacle's bounding box
  if (
    character.x < obstacle.x + obstacle.width &&
    character.x + character.width > obstacle.x &&
    character.y < obstacle.y + obstacle.height &&
    character.y + character.height > obstacle.y
  ) {
    // Collision detected, handle accordingly
  }
}
```

Animation and Feedback

To provide visual feedback to players, animate the character's movement. Change the character's sprite or animation frames as they move in different directions or perform actions.

```javascript
// Example: Animating character movement
function animateCharacterMovement(character, direction) {
  // Change the character's sprite or animation frames based on direction
  character.sprite = /* Load appropriate sprite or animation frames for the direction */;
}
```

Fine-Tuning Controls

It's essential to fine-tune character controls to ensure responsiveness and a satisfying player experience. Consider factors like acceleration, deceleration, and input smoothing to make the movement feel natural and enjoyable.

```javascript
// Example: Implementing character acceleration and deceleration
const maxSpeed = 5; // Maximum movement speed
const acceleration = 0.2; // Acceleration rate
const deceleration = 0.1; // Deceleration rate

let characterSpeed = 0;

function updateCharacterMovement() {
  if (isMovingRight) {
    // Accelerate to the right
    characterSpeed = Math.min(characterSpeed + acceleration, maxSpeed);
  } else if (isMovingLeft) {
    // Accelerate to the left
    characterSpeed = Math.max(characterSpeed - acceleration, -maxSpeed);
  } else {
    // Decelerate when not moving
    if (characterSpeed > 0) {
      characterSpeed = Math.max(characterSpeed - deceleration, 0);
    } else if (characterSpeed < 0) {
      characterSpeed = Math.min(characterSpeed + deceleration, 0);
    }
  }

  // Update character position based on characterSpeed
  character.x += characterSpeed;
}
```

Implementing player character movement and controls requires attention to detail and iteration to ensure a responsive and enjoyable gaming experience. By considering input methods, physics, animation, and control fine-tuning, you can create a character movement system that enhances gameplay in your JavaScript game.

7.3. Creating Interactive Game Objects

In game development, creating interactive game objects is fundamental for building engaging and dynamic gameplay experiences. In this section, we'll explore the process of creating interactive game objects using JavaScript, which can include characters, items, obstacles, and more.

Defining Interactive Game Objects

Interactive game objects are entities within the game world that the player can interact with. These objects can have various properties and behaviors, making them an essential part of game design. When defining interactive game objects, consider the following:

1. **Object Types:** Identify the types of game objects needed in your game. This can include characters, enemies, power-ups, collectibles, doors, switches, and more.

2. **Attributes:** Determine the attributes and properties associated with each game object. For example, a character may have attributes like health, speed, and inventory items.

3. **Behaviors:** Define the behaviors and interactions of game objects. Specify how these objects respond to player input, collisions, and other in-game events.

Object Instantiation and Management

To create interactive game objects in JavaScript, you'll typically use object-oriented programming principles. Here's a simplified example of how you can define and manage game objects using a class-based approach:

```javascript
// Example: Creating a Character class
class Character {
  constructor(name, health, damage) {
    this.name = name;
    this.health = health;
    this.damage = damage;
  }

  // Define methods for character actions
  attack(target) {
    target.takeDamage(this.damage);
  }

  takeDamage(damage) {
    this.health -= damage;
    if (this.health <= 0) {
      // Character is defeated
      this.handleDefeat();
    }
  }

  handleDefeat() {
    // Implement logic for character defeat
  }
}

// Instantiate a character object
```

```
const playerCharacter = new Character('Player', 100, 10);
const enemyCharacter = new Character('Enemy', 80, 8);
```

In this example, we've created a Character class with attributes like name, health, and damage, along with methods for attacking, taking damage, and handling defeat. You can use similar principles to create other interactive game objects.

Object Interactions

Interactive game objects often interact with each other and the player. These interactions can include:

- **Collisions:** Implement collision detection to determine when game objects come into contact. For example, a character colliding with an enemy may trigger combat.

- **Triggers:** Define trigger zones or areas that activate specific actions when entered. For instance, walking into a trigger zone might open a door.

- **Inventory:** Allow game objects to interact with the player's inventory, adding or removing items as needed.

```
// Example: Implementing a trigger zone
class TriggerZone {
  constructor(x, y, width, height, action) {
    this.x = x;
    this.y = y;
    this.width = width;
    this.height = height;
    this.action = action;
  }

  // Check if a character enters the trigger zone
  checkCollision(character) {
    if (
      character.x < this.x + this.width &&
      character.x + character.width > this.x &&
      character.y < this.y + this.height &&
      character.y + character.height > this.y
    ) {
      this.activate(character);
    }
  }

  // Define the action when triggered
  activate(character) {
    // Execute the defined action
    this.action(character);
  }
}
```

In this example, a `TriggerZone` class defines an area that, when entered by a character, triggers a specific action. This allows for a wide range of interactive possibilities in your game.

Implementing Object Variety

To create depth and variety in your game, introduce a diverse set of interactive game objects. Each object should have unique attributes, behaviors, and interactions. This variety keeps players engaged and interested in exploring the game world.

```
// Example: Creating a variety of interactive game objects
const potion = new Item('Health Potion', 'Restores health', 25);
const key = new Item('Silver Key', 'Unlocks doors', null);
const enemyBoss = new Enemy('Boss', 200, 20);
const lever = new InteractiveObject('Lever', 'Opens a gate', () => openGate()
);
```

By defining and managing interactive game objects effectively, you can enhance player engagement and create memorable gaming experiences. Carefully consider the role of each object, its interactions, and its contribution to the overall gameplay.

7.4. User Interface and HUD Elements

User Interface (UI) and Heads-Up Display (HUD) elements play a crucial role in conveying information to players and enhancing their overall gaming experience. In this section, we'll explore the importance of UI and HUD elements in game development and how to implement them using JavaScript.

The Role of UI and HUD

UI elements are graphical components that provide players with information, feedback, and interaction options. HUD elements, on the other hand, are a specific subset of UI elements that are typically displayed on the screen during gameplay, such as health bars, scores, and minimaps.

Here are some key roles of UI and HUD elements in games:

1. **Player Information:** Displaying vital player information, including health, mana, ammunition, and character status.

2. **Objective Tracking:** Indicating current objectives, quest progress, or mission goals.

3. **Game State:** Showing the game's current state, such as paused, menu open, or in combat.

4. **Feedback:** Providing visual and auditory feedback for player actions, interactions, and achievements.

5. **Navigation:** Offering navigation aids like minimaps, waypoints, and compasses for guiding players through the game world.

Implementing UI and HUD elements in JavaScript games involves several steps:

1. **HTML/CSS Integration:** Create HTML elements to represent UI/HUD components and use CSS to style them appropriately. These elements can be positioned on the game screen.

2. **Data Binding:** Connect UI/HUD elements to the underlying game data. For example, link a health bar to the player's health variable.

3. **Event Handling:** Implement event listeners to respond to player interactions with UI components, such as clicking buttons or dragging items.

4. **Update Logic:** Continuously update UI/HUD elements to reflect changes in the game's state. For example, if the player's health decreases, update the health bar accordingly.

5. **Layer Management:** Ensure that UI/HUD elements are correctly layered on top of the game world to prevent interference with gameplay visuals.

```html
<!-- Example HTML structure for a simple HUD with health and score -->
<div id="hud-container">
  <div id="health-bar">
    <div id="health-fill"></div>
  </div>
  <div id="score">Score: <span id="score-value">0</span></div>
</div>
```

```javascript
// Example JavaScript for updating the health bar and score
const healthBar = document.getElementById('health-fill');
const scoreElement = document.getElementById('score-value');

// Update the health bar based on player's health
function updateHealthBar(healthPercentage) {
  healthBar.style.width = healthPercentage + '%';
}

// Update the player's score
function updateScore(newScore) {
  scoreElement.textContent = newScore;
}
```

Design Considerations

When designing UI and HUD elements, consider the following:

1. **Visibility:** Ensure that UI elements are visible and don't obstruct the player's view of the game world.

2. **Consistency:** Maintain a consistent visual style and layout for UI/HUD elements to create a cohesive user experience.

3. **Usability:** Make UI elements intuitive and easy to interact with. Use clear icons and labels.

4. **Performance:** Optimize UI updates to minimize performance impact, especially in fast-paced games.

5. **Responsive Design:** Ensure that UI elements adapt to different screen sizes and orientations, especially in mobile games.

By effectively implementing UI and HUD elements, you can enhance player immersion, provide essential information, and create a more enjoyable gaming experience. Remember to test and iterate on your UI design to find the right balance between functionality and aesthetics.

7.5. Managing Player Health and Inventory

Managing player health and inventory is a critical aspect of game development, as it directly affects gameplay and player experience. In this section, we will delve into how JavaScript can be used to implement and manage these essential elements in your games.

Player Health Management

Player health represents the vitality or well-being of the game character. Here are some key considerations for managing player health:

1. **Health Representation:** Health is often represented as a numerical value or a visual indicator like a health bar. You can use HTML elements and CSS to create health bars, and JavaScript to update them based on the player's health status.

2. **Damage and Healing:** Implement mechanisms for dealing damage to the player (e.g., enemy attacks) and healing (e.g., health potions or medkits). These actions should affect the player's health accordingly.

3. **Game Over Conditions:** Define conditions under which the player's health reaches zero, leading to a game over state. This can trigger various outcomes like restarting the level or displaying a game over screen.

4. **Health Regeneration:** Consider adding health regeneration over time or through specific in-game actions to provide players with opportunities for recovery.

```javascript
// Example JavaScript code for managing player health
let playerHealth = 100; // Initial health value
const healthBar = document.getElementById('health-bar');

// Function to update the health bar
function updateHealthBar() {
  healthBar.style.width = playerHealth + '%';
}

// Function to apply damage to the player
function takeDamage(damageAmount) {
  playerHealth -= damageAmount;

  // Check if the player's health is zero or below
  if (playerHealth <= 0) {
    gameOver();
  }

  updateHealthBar();
}

// Function to heal the player
function healPlayer(healingAmount) {
  playerHealth += healingAmount;

  // Ensure health doesn't exceed the maximum value
  if (playerHealth > 100) {
    playerHealth = 100;
  }

  updateHealthBar();
}

// Function to handle game over
function gameOver() {
  // Implement game over logic here
}
```

Player Inventory Management

Player inventory represents the items, weapons, and resources that a player character carries throughout the game. Proper inventory management is essential for a well-rounded gaming experience:

1. **Inventory System:** Create a data structure (e.g., an array or object) to store player inventory items. Each item should have properties like name, description, quantity, and functionality.

2. **Item Collection:** Implement mechanisms for collecting items, such as picking up objects in the game world or receiving rewards.

3. **Item Usage:** Define how items can be used or consumed in the game. For instance, using a health potion should increase the player's health.

4. **Inventory UI:** Create a user interface to display the player's inventory and allow interaction with items. HTML/CSS can be used to design inventory screens, and JavaScript to manage item interactions.

```javascript
// Example JavaScript code for managing player inventory
const playerInventory = [];

// Function to add an item to the player's inventory
function addItemToInventory(item) {
  playerInventory.push(item);
}

// Function to remove an item from the player's inventory
function removeItemFromInventory(item) {
  const index = playerInventory.indexOf(item);
  if (index !== -1) {
    playerInventory.splice(index, 1);
  }
}

// Example item usage function (e.g., using a health potion)
function useHealthPotion() {
  const healthPotion = playerInventory.find((item) => item.name === 'Health P
otion');
  if (healthPotion) {
    healPlayer(healthPotion.healingAmount);
    removeItemFromInventory(healthPotion);
  }
}

// Example item object
const healthPotionItem = {
  name: 'Health Potion',
  description: 'Restores health',
  healingAmount: 30,
};

addItemToInventory(healthPotionItem);
```

Effective management of player health and inventory enhances gameplay dynamics and allows players to strategize based on their resources. Ensure that your game's balance and challenge factor in these elements for an engaging experience.

103

Chapter 8: AI and Enemy Behavior

8.1. Basics of Game AI

Game Artificial Intelligence (AI) plays a crucial role in creating dynamic and challenging gameplay experiences. In this section, we will explore the fundamentals of implementing game AI using JavaScript.

What is Game AI?

Game AI refers to the algorithms and logic that control non-player characters (NPCs) and entities in a game. These entities can include enemies, allies, and neutral characters. The primary goals of game AI are to make NPCs act intelligently, respond to the player's actions, and provide engaging challenges.

Key Components of Game AI:

1. Decision-Making:
- NPCs need to make decisions based on the game's context and their role. This includes choosing actions, targets, and strategies.
- Decision trees, state machines, and behavior trees are common approaches to decision-making in game AI.

2. Pathfinding:
- Pathfinding algorithms help NPCs navigate the game world efficiently. Common algorithms include A* (A-star) and Dijkstra's algorithm.
- Grid-based or navigation mesh-based systems are used to represent the game world for pathfinding.

3. Behavior Patterns:
- NPCs exhibit various behavior patterns, such as chasing the player, patrolling a designated area, or fleeing when low on health.
- Finite state machines (FSM) and scripting are often used to define behavior patterns.

4. Sensing and Perception:
- NPCs need to perceive the game environment and the player's actions. This includes detecting the player's presence, hearing sounds, and recognizing objects.
- Sensors and perception systems are essential for creating responsive AI.

JavaScript for Game AI:

JavaScript provides a flexible and powerful platform for implementing game AI due to its ease of use and compatibility with web-based games. Here are some key considerations when using JavaScript for game AI:

- **State Management:** Use JavaScript to manage the state of NPCs. Each state represents a specific behavior or action, and NPCs transition between states based on conditions.

- **Event Handling:** JavaScript's event handling capabilities are handy for responding to player actions or in-game events. For example, detecting when the player enters an NPC's line of sight.

- **Math and Physics:** JavaScript's built-in math functions and libraries can be used for calculations like distance checks, angle calculations, and physics simulations.

- **Optimization:** Ensure that your AI code is optimized for performance, especially in real-time games. Implement techniques like spatial partitioning to reduce the number of AI calculations.

- **Testing and Debugging:** Use JavaScript's debugging tools to test and fine-tune your AI behaviors. Visualize AI decisions and paths for easier debugging.

- **Learning AI:** Consider implementing machine learning techniques for more advanced AI behaviors. Reinforcement learning and neural networks can be used to create adaptive NPCs.

```javascript
// Example JavaScript code for a simple state-based NPC AI
class NPC {
  constructor() {
    this.state = 'idle';
  }

  update() {
    // AI logic based on the current state
    switch (this.state) {
      case 'idle':
        // Perform idle behavior
        break;
      case 'chasing':
        // Perform chasing behavior
        break;
      case 'attacking':
        // Perform attacking behavior
        break;
      default:
        // Handle unexpected state
    }
  }

  setState(newState) {
    // Transition to a new AI state
    this.state = newState;
  }
}
```

```
}
```

```
// Usage
const enemyNPC = new NPC();
enemyNPC.setState('chasing');
enemyNPC.update();
```

Implementing game AI in JavaScript requires creativity and an understanding of player expectations. Whether you're creating challenging enemies or friendly NPCs, effective AI can significantly enhance the gaming experience.

8.2. Pathfinding and Movement Algorithms

In the realm of game AI, pathfinding and movement algorithms are essential tools for NPCs to navigate through complex game worlds. This section will delve into the basics of pathfinding and movement algorithms used in game development, particularly focusing on JavaScript implementations.

Understanding Pathfinding

Pathfinding is the process of finding the most optimal path from one location to another within a game world, taking into account obstacles, terrain, and other factors. NPCs and characters, such as enemies or allies, rely on pathfinding to move intelligently and reach their intended destinations.

Common Pathfinding Algorithms

1. _A_ Algorithm:_* A* (pronounced "A-star") is a popular and versatile pathfinding algorithm that guarantees the shortest path. It uses a combination of heuristics and cost calculations to prioritize the most promising paths, making it efficient for various game scenarios.

2. **Dijkstra's Algorithm:** Dijkstra's algorithm finds the shortest path by exploring all possible routes systematically. While not as efficient as A* in most cases, it guarantees the shortest path without any heuristics.

3. **Breadth-First Search (BFS):** BFS explores neighboring nodes before moving to more distant ones. It's simple and effective for uniform-cost grids but may not be suitable for more complex environments.

4. **Depth-First Search (DFS):** DFS explores as far as possible along each branch before backtracking. It's not typically used for pathfinding due to its lack of guarantee for the shortest path, but it has applications in other areas of game development.

Implementing Pathfinding in JavaScript

JavaScript offers several libraries and tools for implementing pathfinding in your games:

106

- **Pathfinding.js:** A JavaScript library that provides various pathfinding algorithms, including A* and Dijkstra's, for 2D grids.

- **Phaser:** A popular game framework for JavaScript that includes built-in support for pathfinding and movement components.

- **Three.js:** If you're working with 3D games, Three.js can be used to implement pathfinding in a 3D environment.

Here's a simplified example of using the A* algorithm in JavaScript to find a path on a grid:

```javascript
// Example A* pathfinding algorithm in JavaScript
function findPath(start, target, grid) {
  const openSet = [start];
  const cameFrom = {};

  const gScore = {}; // Cost from start to current node
  gScore[start] = 0;

  const fScore = {}; // Estimated total cost from start to target
  fScore[start] = heuristic(start, target);

  while (openSet.length > 0) {
    const current = findLowestFScore(openSet, fScore);

    if (current === target) {
      return reconstructPath(cameFrom, current);
    }

    openSet.splice(openSet.indexOf(current), 1);

    const neighbors = getNeighbors(current, grid);

    for (const neighbor of neighbors) {
      const tentativeGScore = gScore[current] + distance(current, neighbor);

      if (tentativeGScore < gScore[neighbor] || gScore[neighbor] === undefined) {
        cameFrom[neighbor] = current;
        gScore[neighbor] = tentativeGScore;
        fScore[neighbor] = gScore[neighbor] + heuristic(neighbor, target);

        if (!openSet.includes(neighbor)) {
          openSet.push(neighbor);
        }
      }
    }
  }
}
```

```
    return null; // No path found
}
```

Implementing pathfinding and movement algorithms is crucial for creating believable and interactive NPCs in your games. These algorithms enable characters to navigate the game world efficiently, avoid obstacles, and interact with the player and environment intelligently.

8.3. Enemy Design and Behavior Patterns

In the realm of game development, creating engaging and challenging enemy behavior is crucial for player immersion and enjoyment. This section explores enemy design and behavior patterns in JavaScript game development, providing insights into how to craft formidable foes for your games.

Designing Enemies

Before delving into behavior patterns, it's essential to consider enemy design. Factors to contemplate include:

1. **Visual Appearance:** Enemies should be visually distinct from the player character and other elements in the game. Clear visual cues help players identify threats quickly.

2. **Variety:** Introduce a variety of enemy types with unique appearances, abilities, and weaknesses. This keeps the gameplay fresh and engaging.

3. **Weaknesses:** Every enemy should have exploitable weaknesses that players can discover and leverage. This adds depth to combat mechanics.

4. **Scaling Difficulty:** Design enemies that scale in difficulty as players progress through the game. Early encounters should be less challenging than later ones.

Common Enemy Behavior Patterns

1. **Aggression:** Aggressive enemies actively seek out the player character and attack on sight. They might use melee or ranged attacks and pursue the player relentlessly.

2. **Patrolling:** Patrolling enemies follow predefined paths, periodically stopping and scanning their surroundings for the player. They provide opportunities for stealth and strategic gameplay.

3. **Stationary:** Stationary enemies remain in fixed positions but have a ranged attack or other abilities. They create obstacles that players must navigate around or eliminate.

4. **Swarming:** Swarm behavior involves groups of enemies that coordinate their actions, overwhelming the player with numbers. Cooperation and tactics are key to defeating them.

5. **Boss Fights:** Boss enemies are usually larger and more powerful than standard foes. Boss fights often have multiple phases, each with different attack patterns and vulnerabilities.

Implementing Enemy Behavior in JavaScript

Implementing enemy behavior in JavaScript typically involves state machines, decision trees, or behavior trees. These structures manage an enemy's actions based on its current state and conditions. Here's a simplified example of a state machine for a patrolling enemy:

```javascript
// Example enemy state machine in JavaScript
class Enemy {
  constructor() {
    this.state = 'patrol';
  }

  update(playerPosition) {
    switch (this.state) {
      case 'patrol':
        this.patrol();
        if (this.detectPlayer(playerPosition)) {
          this.state = 'chase';
        }
        break;

      case 'chase':
        this.chase(playerPosition);
        if (!this.detectPlayer(playerPosition)) {
          this.state = 'patrol';
        }
        break;
    }
  }

  patrol() {
    // Implement patrolling behavior here
  }

  chase(playerPosition) {
    // Implement chasing behavior here
  }

  detectPlayer(playerPosition) {
    // Implement player detection logic here
```

```
    }
}
```

This simple state machine switches between patrolling and chasing states based on the player's presence. More complex behaviors can be implemented by expanding the state machine or using other AI techniques.

Creating compelling enemy behavior is an art that combines game design principles with programming skills. Effective enemies challenge players, enhance immersion, and contribute significantly to the overall gaming experience.

8.4. Implementing AI Decision Making

Artificial Intelligence (AI) is an essential component of modern game development, contributing to realistic and engaging gameplay experiences. In this section, we'll explore the implementation of AI decision-making processes in JavaScript games.

The Role of AI Decision Making

AI decision making determines how NPCs (Non-Player Characters) and entities in a game interact with the game world and players. It involves analyzing the current game state, evaluating various actions, and selecting the most appropriate course of action.

Key Components of AI Decision Making

1. **Perception:** AI entities must perceive the game world to make informed decisions. This includes detecting and interpreting relevant information, such as the player's position, nearby obstacles, and other NPCs.

2. **Goal Setting:** AI needs specific objectives or goals. These goals guide decision-making, helping AI entities prioritize actions that bring them closer to achieving their objectives.

3. **Decision Logic:** Decision logic consists of algorithms and rules that AI entities use to evaluate their options. These rules can be as simple as "attack the player if in range" or as complex as a decision tree.

4. **State Machines:** State machines help model AI behavior by defining different states and transitions between them. States represent different AI behaviors (e.g., idle, chase, attack), and transitions occur based on conditions or events.

Example: Enemy AI Decision Making

Let's consider a simplified example of implementing AI decision making for an enemy that decides whether to chase, attack, or flee from the player.

```
class EnemyAI {
  constructor(enemy, player) {
    this.enemy = enemy;
    this.player = player;
  }

  makeDecision() {
    const distanceToPlayer = calculateDistance(this.enemy.position, this.play
er.position);

    if (distanceToPlayer < 10) {
      if (this.enemy.health < 30) {
        this.enemy.flee();
      } else {
        this.enemy.attack(this.player);
      }
    } else {
      this.enemy.chase(this.player);
    }
  }
}
```

In this example, the makeDecision function assesses the distance to the player and the enemy's health. If the player is nearby and the enemy's health is low, it decides to flee; otherwise, it attacks the player. If the player is not nearby, it chooses to chase.

Advanced Techniques

For more complex AI behaviors, developers may employ techniques such as behavior trees, neural networks, and pathfinding algorithms. These methods allow for sophisticated decision-making processes that adapt to changing game situations.

Implementing AI decision making in games is a creative and challenging task. It requires a balance between realism and fun, as well as a deep understanding of game design and programming. Effective AI can enhance the player's experience by creating challenging and immersive gameplay scenarios.

8.5. Balancing Difficulty and AI Complexity

Balancing difficulty and AI complexity is a critical aspect of game development. Achieving the right level of challenge and providing an engaging experience for players is essential for a successful game. In this section, we'll explore the concepts and strategies for balancing AI complexity and difficulty.

Understanding Difficulty Levels

Games often feature multiple difficulty levels, catering to a wide range of players, from beginners to experts. These difficulty levels influence various aspects of gameplay, including enemy AI behavior, player character abilities, and resource availability. Players can choose the difficulty level that best suits their skill and preference.

Factors Influencing AI Complexity

1. **Player Skill:** Consider the skill level of your target audience. Novice players may prefer simpler and more predictable AI, while experienced gamers may seek challenging opponents.

2. **Game Genre:** The genre of your game influences AI complexity. Strategy games may require sophisticated AI for strategic decision-making, while platformers may focus on precise movement and simple behaviors.

3. **Progression:** AI complexity can vary as players progress through the game. Early levels may feature basic enemies, while later stages introduce more intelligent and challenging foes.

Strategies for Balancing AI Complexity

1. **Difficulty Levels:** Implement multiple difficulty levels, allowing players to choose their preferred challenge. Adjust AI behavior, damage values, and enemy statistics accordingly.

2. **Dynamic Scaling:** Implement dynamic scaling of AI based on player performance. If a player is struggling, AI difficulty can decrease, and vice versa.

3. **Player Feedback:** Collect player feedback and analytics to assess difficulty balance. This data can help you make informed adjustments.

4. **Testing and Iteration:** Thoroughly playtest your game with a diverse group of players to identify difficulty issues. Iterate on AI behaviors and mechanics based on player feedback.

Example: Difficulty Levels in a Shooter Game

```
class ShooterGame {
  constructor(player, enemies) {
    this.player = player;
    this.enemies = enemies;
    this.difficulty = 'normal';
  }

  setDifficulty(difficulty) {
    this.difficulty = difficulty;
    // Adjust AI behavior, enemy health, and other parameters based on diffic
ulty.
    if (difficulty === 'easy') {
      // Simplify AI behavior.
```

```
        this.enemies.forEach(enemy => enemy.simplifyAI());
      } else if (difficulty === 'hard') {
        // Make AI more challenging.
        this.enemies.forEach(enemy => enemy.boostAI());
      }
    }
  }
}
```

In this example, the ShooterGame class allows players to set the game's difficulty level. Depending on the chosen difficulty, AI behavior is adjusted to provide an appropriate level of challenge.

Balancing AI complexity and difficulty is an ongoing process in game development. Continuous testing, player feedback, and adjustments are crucial to ensure an enjoyable gaming experience for all players, regardless of their skill level.

9.1. Understanding WebSockets for Real-Time Gaming

Real-time multiplayer games require a robust and efficient communication system to synchronize game states and handle player interactions. WebSockets have become a popular choice for implementing real-time communication in web-based games. In this section, we'll explore WebSockets and how they can be used for real-time gaming.

What Are WebSockets?

WebSockets are a protocol that provides full-duplex communication channels over a single TCP connection. Unlike traditional HTTP requests, which are stateless and require the client to initiate each interaction, WebSockets establish a persistent connection that allows bidirectional data exchange between the client (usually a web browser) and the server.

Advantages of WebSockets in Gaming

1. **Low Latency:** WebSockets offer low-latency communication, making them ideal for real-time gaming where timely updates are crucial.

2. **Efficiency:** WebSockets reduce overhead compared to traditional HTTP requests, as they eliminate the need for headers and reestablishing connections.

3. **Full Duplex:** WebSockets enable both the server and client to send data simultaneously, facilitating real-time synchronization.

Implementing WebSockets in JavaScript

To use WebSockets in JavaScript, you can utilize the WebSocket API provided by modern web browsers. Here's a basic example of setting up a WebSocket connection in a web-based game:

```javascript
// Client-side WebSocket setup
const socket = new WebSocket('ws://example.com/game');

socket.addEventListener('open', () => {
  console.log('WebSocket connection established');
});

socket.addEventListener('message', (event) => {
  const data = JSON.parse(event.data);
  // Handle incoming game data here.
});

socket.addEventListener('close', (event) => {
  if (event.wasClean) {
    console.log(`WebSocket connection closed cleanly, code=${event.code}, reason=${event.reason}`);
  } else {
    console.error('Connection abruptly closed');
  }
});

socket.addEventListener('error', (error) => {
  console.error(`WebSocket error: ${error.message}`);
});
```

Server-Side WebSocket Implementation

On the server side, you'll need a WebSocket server to handle incoming connections and manage WebSocket sessions. Various libraries and frameworks are available in different programming languages to simplify WebSocket server implementation.

Real-Time Game Features

WebSockets can be used to implement various real-time features in games, including:

- Player movement and position synchronization.
- Sending game events such as player actions, collisions, and item pickups.
- Chat systems for in-game communication.
- Real-time leaderboards and game statistics updates.

When implementing WebSockets in your game, it's crucial to consider security measures to prevent cheating and unauthorized access to the game server.

WebSockets have revolutionized the way real-time multiplayer games are developed for the web. They provide the necessary tools for creating engaging and interactive gaming experiences where players can compete or collaborate in real time. Understanding WebSockets is essential for game developers looking to build multiplayer web-based games that offer a seamless and responsive gameplay experience.

9.2. Building a Basic Multiplayer Game Framework

In the previous section, we discussed the fundamentals of WebSockets and their role in real-time gaming. Now, let's dive into building a basic multiplayer game framework using WebSockets in JavaScript. This framework will serve as a starting point for developing your own real-time multiplayer games.

Setting Up the Project

Before we start coding, ensure you have Node.js and npm (Node Package Manager) installed on your development machine. You'll also need a code editor of your choice.

1. Create a new directory for your project and navigate to it in your terminal.

2. Run the following command to initialize a new Node.js project and create a `package.json` file:

   ```
   npm init -y
   ```

3. Install the ws (WebSocket) library by running:

   ```
   npm install ws
   ```

Creating a WebSocket Server

We'll begin by setting up a WebSocket server that handles incoming connections from players. Create a file named `server.js` in your project directory and add the following code:

```js
const WebSocket = require('ws');
const wss = new WebSocket.Server({ port: 8080 }); // WebSocket server listens
on port 8080

// Store connected clients
const clients = new Set();

// Handle incoming connections
wss.on('connection', (ws) => {
  clients.add(ws);
  console.log('Client connected');

  // Handle incoming messages
  ws.on('message', (message) => {
    // Broadcast the message to all connected clients
    wss.clients.forEach((client) => {
      if (client !== ws && client.readyState === WebSocket.OPEN) {
        client.send(message);
      }
```

```
    });
  });

  // Handle client disconnection
  ws.on('close', () => {
    clients.delete(ws);
    console.log('Client disconnected');
  });
});

console.log('WebSocket server is running on port 8080');
```

Creating a Simple HTML Client

Next, create an HTML file named index.html in your project directory to serve as the game client. This simple client will allow players to connect to the server and exchange messages. Add the following code to index.html:

```html
<!DOCTYPE html>
<html lang="en">
<head>
    <meta charset="UTF-8">
    <meta name="viewport" content="width=device-width, initial-scale=1.0">
    <title>Basic Multiplayer Game</title>
</head>
<body>
    <h1>Basic Multiplayer Game</h1>
    <textarea id="message" placeholder="Enter your message"></textarea>
    <button id="send">Send</button>
    <div id="output"></div>

    <script>
        const ws = new WebSocket('ws://localhost:8080'); // WebSocket connection to the server

        const messageInput = document.getElementById('message');
        const sendButton = document.getElementById('send');
        const outputDiv = document.getElementById('output');

        sendButton.addEventListener('click', () => {
            const message = messageInput.value;
            ws.send(message);
            messageInput.value = '';
        });

        ws.addEventListener('message', (event) => {
            const message = event.data;
            outputDiv.innerHTML += `<p>${message}</p>`;
        });
    </script>
```

116

```
</body>
</html>
```

Now that you've set up the server and client, follow these steps to run the basic multiplayer game:

1. Open your terminal and navigate to your project directory.

2. Start the WebSocket server by running:

    `node server.js`

3. Open a web browser and go to `http://localhost:8080` to access the client. You can open multiple browser tabs/windows to simulate multiple players.

4. Players can enter messages in the text area and click the "Send" button to exchange messages with each other in real-time.

This basic framework provides a foundation for building more complex real-time multiplayer games using WebSockets in JavaScript. You can extend it by adding game-specific logic, handling player positions, and implementing game mechanics.

9.3. Managing Player Connections and Data

In a multiplayer game, managing player connections and data is a crucial aspect of creating a seamless and enjoyable gaming experience. In this section, we'll explore how to handle player connections, maintain player data, and ensure synchronization between clients and the server.

Player Authentication and Identification

When players connect to a multiplayer game, it's essential to authenticate and identify them. This helps in tracking player progress, enforcing security measures, and providing a personalized gaming experience.

Authentication:

Player authentication can be achieved through various methods, such as username and password, OAuth, or token-based authentication. Ensure that your authentication process is secure to prevent unauthorized access to your game.

Identification:

Each player should have a unique identifier, often referred to as a player ID or session ID. This identifier helps in distinguishing players and associating them with their in-game data.

Player Data Storage

To maintain player progress, game state, and other relevant information, you need a reliable storage mechanism. Here are some common approaches to store player data:

Databases:

Using databases like MySQL, MongoDB, or Redis, you can store player profiles, achievements, scores, and game state. Databases offer flexibility and scalability for handling player data.

In-Memory Storage:

For real-time interactions and faster data access, you can use in-memory storage solutions like Redis. In-memory storage is particularly useful for temporary game data and leaderboards.

Cloud Storage:

Cloud storage services such as Amazon S3 or Google Cloud Storage are suitable for storing game assets, player avatars, and other multimedia elements.

Synchronizing Player Actions

In a multiplayer game, player actions need to be synchronized across all connected clients to maintain a consistent game state. Here are key considerations for achieving synchronization:

Real-Time Communication:

Utilize WebSocket or other real-time communication protocols to transmit player actions and game updates instantly. WebSocket enables bidirectional communication between clients and the server.

Server Authority:

The server should have the final authority over the game state to prevent cheating and ensure fair gameplay. Players' actions are validated and processed on the server before being broadcasted to others.

Handling Disconnects and Reconnections

Players may disconnect from the game due to network issues, leaving the game, or other reasons. Managing disconnects and reconnections is essential for maintaining game integrity:

Disconnection Handling:

When a player disconnects, the server should handle it gracefully. The player's state and progress should be preserved, and other players should be notified of the disconnection.

Support player reconnection by allowing disconnected players to resume their game sessions. Ensure that the reconnected player's data is synchronized with the current game state.

Player Interaction and Communication

Facilitate player interaction and communication by providing features like chat systems, in-game messaging, and friend requests. These features enhance the social aspect of multiplayer gaming.

Chat Systems:

Implement chat systems that allow players to send messages, both privately and in group chats. This fosters communication and cooperation among players.

In-Game Messaging:

Enable in-game messaging for sending game-related information and notifications to players. It helps in conveying important updates and events.

Friend Requests:

Allow players to send and accept friend requests, making it easier to connect with other players and form teams or groups.

Security and Privacy

Maintaining the security and privacy of player data is paramount. Implement security measures to protect player accounts, sensitive information, and ensure a safe gaming environment:

Encryption:

Encrypt data transmitted between clients and the server to prevent eavesdropping and data tampering. Use secure communication protocols like HTTPS and WSS (WebSocket Secure).

Privacy Policies:

Clearly communicate your game's privacy policies to players, including data collection, usage, and storage practices. Comply with relevant data protection regulations, such as GDPR.

Conclusion

Managing player connections and data is a multifaceted aspect of multiplayer game development. By ensuring secure authentication, robust data storage, synchronization of player actions, handling disconnects and reconnections, facilitating player communication, and prioritizing security and privacy, you can create a captivating and enjoyable multiplayer gaming experience for your players.

9.4. Synchronizing Game States

Synchronizing game states is a critical aspect of multiplayer game development. It ensures that all players are experiencing the same game world and that actions taken by one player are reflected in real-time for all others. In this section, we will explore various techniques and strategies for synchronizing game states effectively.

Server Authority

In a multiplayer game, the server should have the ultimate authority over the game state. This means that all critical game logic, such as character movement, combat resolution, and item interactions, should be processed on the server. Clients can send their inputs and commands to the server, which then validates and processes them before updating the game state and broadcasting it back to all connected clients. This approach prevents cheating and ensures fairness.

Game State Replication

To synchronize game states across all clients, you can use a replication system. Here's how it works:

1. **Server State:** The server maintains the authoritative game state. This includes the positions and states of all game objects, player characters, NPCs, and other relevant data.

2. **Client State:** Each client also maintains a local game state that mirrors the server's state. This state is used for rendering and predicting game object movements to reduce perceived latency.

3. **State Updates:** The server periodically sends state updates to all clients. These updates contain information about the current state of the game, including changes in object positions, status updates, and new events.

4. **Client Interpolation:** Clients interpolate between state updates to smooth out movement and animations, making the game appear fluid even with varying network latencies.

Network Latency Compensation

Network latency can introduce delays between a player's action and its effect on the game state. To compensate for latency, you can employ techniques such as client-side prediction and server reconciliation:

1. **Client-Side Prediction:** Clients predict the outcome of their actions locally before receiving updates from the server. This means that when a player moves their character, the client immediately shows the movement, even before the server confirms it. If the server's response contradicts the prediction, the client corrects its state to match the server's.

2. **Server Reconciliation:** After receiving input from a client, the server may process the input with a slight delay to account for network latency. This delay allows the server to reconcile any discrepancies between the client's predicted state and the authoritative server state.

State Serialization

To send and receive game states efficiently, you need to serialize game data into a format that can be transmitted over the network. Popular formats for serialization include JSON, Protocol Buffers, and binary formats. It's essential to optimize the size of serialized data to minimize network bandwidth usage and reduce latency.

Bandwidth Optimization

Minimizing the amount of data sent over the network is crucial for maintaining a responsive multiplayer experience, especially for players with slower connections. Some bandwidth optimization techniques include:

- **Delta Compression:** Send only the changes in the game state between updates instead of sending the entire state each time.
- **Entity Interpolation:** Interpolate object positions and movements smoothly between updates to reduce jerky movements caused by low update rates.
- **Data Compression:** Use data compression algorithms to further reduce the size of network packets.
- **Rate Limiting:** Control the rate at which updates are sent to clients to prevent flooding the network with data.

Conclusion

Synchronizing game states in multiplayer games is a complex but essential task. By giving the server authority, implementing a robust replication system, compensating for network latency, optimizing state serialization, and minimizing network bandwidth usage, you can create a multiplayer gaming experience that is enjoyable, fair, and responsive for all players.

9.5. Security and Cheating Prevention in Online Games

Ensuring the security and fairness of online multiplayer games is crucial to providing an enjoyable experience for all players. Cheating can ruin the experience and undermine the integrity of the game. In this section, we will explore various techniques and strategies for securing your online game and preventing cheating.

Server-Side Validation

One of the most critical aspects of cheating prevention is server-side validation. This means that the server should validate all actions and inputs from clients before accepting them as valid. Here are some key points to consider:

- **Input Validation:** The server should validate and sanitize all input data received from clients, including player actions, to ensure that it is within the expected parameters and does not contain malicious code.

- **Authority:** As mentioned earlier, the server should have the ultimate authority over the game state. This includes verifying actions such as player movement, combat outcomes, and item interactions. Client actions should be treated as requests that the server can accept, reject, or modify as necessary.

- **Anti-Cheat Measures:** Implement anti-cheat mechanisms on the server to detect and prevent common cheating techniques, such as aimbots, wallhacks, and speed hacks. These mechanisms can include server-side checks for abnormal behavior and the use of cheat detection libraries.

Data Encryption

Encrypting sensitive data transmitted between clients and servers is essential to prevent eavesdropping and tampering. Here are some encryption techniques to consider:

- **Secure Sockets Layer (SSL) / Transport Layer Security (TLS):** Use SSL/TLS to encrypt data transmitted over the network, such as login credentials, player data, and game state updates. This ensures that data remains confidential and cannot be intercepted easily.

- **Data Packet Encryption:** Encrypt individual data packets exchanged between clients and servers. This can include using encryption libraries to secure the content of messages.

Player Authentication

Implement robust player authentication mechanisms to ensure that only legitimate players can access your game:

- **Account Registration:** Require players to create accounts with unique usernames and strong passwords. Implement email verification to confirm the authenticity of registered email addresses.

- **Two-Factor Authentication (2FA):** Offer 2FA as an additional layer of security. This can involve sending one-time codes to players' mobile devices or email addresses.

- **Login Rate Limiting:** Implement rate limiting for login attempts to prevent brute-force attacks on player accounts. Lock accounts temporarily after multiple failed login attempts.

To maintain game fairness and detect suspicious behavior, consider the following:

- **Behavior Monitoring:** Use behavior monitoring systems to track player actions and identify unusual or suspicious patterns. This can include tracking statistics like kill-to-death ratios and win percentages.

- **Reporting Mechanisms:** Implement an in-game reporting system that allows players to report suspected cheaters or abusive behavior. Investigate reported cases and take appropriate actions.

Stay vigilant and release regular updates to your game to address security vulnerabilities and known cheats. Keeping the game client and server software up to date is crucial for staying ahead of cheaters who may exploit older versions.

Preventing cheating in online games is an ongoing battle, but with the right strategies and technologies, you can create a more secure and enjoyable gaming environment for your players. By implementing server-side validation, data encryption, player authentication, fairness monitoring, and regular updates, you can significantly reduce the risk of cheating and maintain the integrity of your online multiplayer game.

Chapter 10: Mobile Game Development

Mobile game development has become increasingly popular due to the widespread use of smartphones and tablets. In this chapter, we'll explore the key aspects of adapting your games for mobile platforms. We'll cover topics such as touch controls, responsive design, accessing device features, and the process of publishing and monetizing your mobile games.

10.1. Adapting Games for Mobile Platforms

Adapting your game for mobile platforms requires careful consideration of various factors to ensure an optimal user experience. Here are some key points to keep in mind when porting your game to mobile:

1. User Interface (UI) and Controls

Mobile devices have smaller screens and different input methods compared to desktop computers or consoles. Therefore, it's essential to redesign your game's user interface and controls to be touch-friendly and intuitive.

- **Touch Controls:** Implement touch controls for actions like tapping, swiping, and pinching. Ensure that buttons and icons are large enough to be easily tapped by users of all ages.

- **Gestures:** Take advantage of gestures to enhance gameplay. For example, swipe gestures for character movement or pinch gestures for zooming in and out.

- **Virtual Joysticks:** If your game requires virtual joysticks or D-pads for precise control, design them to be responsive and customizable by the player.

2. Screen Resolutions and Aspect Ratios

Mobile devices come in various screen sizes, resolutions, and aspect ratios. Your game should adapt seamlessly to different devices to avoid letterboxing or stretching.

- **Responsive Design:** Implement responsive design principles to ensure that your game's graphics and UI elements scale and adjust appropriately to different screen sizes and orientations.

- **Asset Scaling:** Create multiple sets of assets (sprites, textures, UI elements) at different resolutions to maintain visual quality across devices.

3. Performance Optimization

Mobile devices have limited processing power and memory compared to desktop computers. Optimize your game's performance to run smoothly on a wide range of devices.

- **Graphics Settings:** Allow players to adjust graphics settings to find the right balance between visual quality and performance.

- **Memory Management:** Implement efficient memory management to avoid crashes or slowdowns due to memory exhaustion.

4. Battery Consumption

Mobile games should be mindful of battery life. Constantly running background processes or high-intensity graphics can drain a device's battery quickly.

- **Background Processes:** Minimize background processes when the game is not in use. Pause or reduce resource-intensive tasks when the game is in the background.

- **Energy-Efficient Code:** Write energy-efficient code to reduce CPU and GPU usage, which can help extend battery life.

5. Device Features

Leverage the unique features of mobile devices to enhance gameplay and engagement.

- **Accelerometer:** Use the accelerometer to detect device movement for games like racing or tilt-based puzzles.

- **GPS and Location:** Incorporate GPS and location data for location-based gameplay or augmented reality features.

- **Camera:** Utilize the camera for AR experiences or for taking in-game photos.

6. Testing on Real Devices

Testing your game on real mobile devices is crucial to identifying and resolving issues specific to various platforms and hardware configurations.

- **Device Variety:** Test on a variety of Android and iOS devices to ensure compatibility.

- **Beta Testing:** Conduct beta testing with a group of players to gather feedback and identify any issues that may arise.

7. Cross-Platform Development

Consider using cross-platform development frameworks and tools that allow you to develop your game for both Android and iOS simultaneously, saving time and effort.

- **Unity:** Unity is a popular game engine that supports cross-platform development, making it easier to target multiple mobile platforms.

Adapting your game for mobile platforms can be a rewarding endeavor, as it opens up a vast and diverse audience of potential players. By addressing the specific challenges and opportunities presented by mobile devices, you can create engaging and successful mobile games.

10.2. Touch Controls and Mobile Interfaces

Mobile game development requires careful consideration of touch controls and the design of mobile interfaces. Unlike traditional gaming platforms, mobile devices rely on touchscreens as the primary input method. In this section, we'll explore best practices for implementing touch controls and creating intuitive mobile interfaces for your games.

1. Responsive Touch Controls

- **Touch Targets:** Ensure that on-screen buttons, icons, and controls are appropriately sized for touch input. Small touch targets can frustrate players, leading to a poor user experience.

- **Gestures:** Implement swipe gestures, pinch-to-zoom, and other touch gestures to provide players with intuitive ways to interact with the game. For example, swipe left and right for character movement or pinch to zoom in on maps.

- **Virtual Joysticks:** When designing virtual joysticks or D-pads, make them responsive and customizable. Allow players to adjust the joystick's size and sensitivity to match their preferences.

2. On-Screen Buttons and HUD

- **Minimize Clutter:** Avoid overcrowding the screen with on-screen buttons and HUD elements. Keep the interface clean and unobtrusive to provide players with an immersive gaming experience.

- **Contextual Buttons:** Use contextual buttons that appear when needed and disappear when not in use. For example, display an "Attack" button when the player approaches an enemy.

- **Customizable HUD:** Allow players to customize the heads-up display (HUD) to their liking. They may want to reposition or resize HUD elements based on their preferences.

3. Multi-Touch Support

- **Multi-Touch Actions:** Some games benefit from multi-touch support, allowing players to perform multiple actions simultaneously. For instance, in a strategy game, a player might zoom in on the map with one finger while selecting units with another.

- **Pinch and Zoom:** Implement pinch-to-zoom functionality for games with zoomable maps or environments. Ensure that zooming feels smooth and responsive.

4. Feedback and Visual Cues

- **Visual Feedback:** Provide visual cues to indicate touch interactions, such as button presses or swipe directions. Visual feedback helps players understand the consequences of their actions.

- **Audio Feedback:** Consider using audio feedback, such as button click sounds or character voice lines, to enhance the overall gaming experience.

5. Testing and User Feedback

- **Usability Testing:** Conduct usability testing with real players to identify any issues with touch controls and interface design. Collect feedback on the intuitiveness of controls and adjust as needed.

- **Iterative Design:** Be prepared to iterate on your game's touch controls and interface based on user feedback. Continuously improving the mobile interface can lead to higher player satisfaction.

6. Accessibility

- **Accessibility Features:** Ensure that your game's touch controls and interfaces are accessible to players with disabilities. Consider features such as customizable button sizes, high-contrast modes, and support for screen readers.

- **User Testing with Accessibility in Mind:** Include players with disabilities in your user testing sessions to gather valuable insights and make necessary adjustments.

7. Tutorials and Onboarding

- **Guided Onboarding:** Implement guided tutorials and onboarding sequences to introduce players to the touch controls and mobile interface. Gradually introduce complex interactions to avoid overwhelming new players.

- **In-Game Help:** Provide in-game help or tooltips that explain the function of on-screen buttons and gestures, especially if they have unique or non-standard uses.

8. Optimizing for Different Devices

- **Device Fragmentation:** Consider the wide range of Android and iOS devices with varying screen sizes and resolutions. Test your touch controls on different devices to ensure consistent performance and usability.

Implementing effective touch controls and designing mobile interfaces that prioritize user experience is crucial for the success of your mobile game. By following these best practices and continuously gathering user feedback, you can create a mobile gaming experience that resonates with players and keeps them engaged.

10.3. Responsive Design and Mobile Optimization

Mobile game development not only involves adapting gameplay and controls but also optimizing your game for a variety of mobile devices. In this section, we will explore the importance of responsive design and mobile optimization to ensure that your game runs smoothly and looks great on different smartphones and tablets.

1. Device Diversity

Mobile devices come in various screen sizes, resolutions, and aspect ratios. To accommodate this diversity:

- **Aspect Ratio Handling:** Design your game to support different aspect ratios, including 16:9, 18:9, and others. Use responsive layouts that adjust to fit the screen without distorting the game's visuals.

- **Screen Sizes:** Test your game on various screen sizes, from smaller smartphones to larger tablets. Ensure that user interface elements are appropriately sized and spaced for each device.

2. Performance Optimization

- **Graphics Optimization:** Optimize textures, models, and shaders for mobile performance. Use texture compression formats like ETC2 and ASTC to reduce memory usage and improve loading times.

- **Frame Rate:** Target a consistent frame rate, such as 30 or 60 frames per second (FPS), depending on your game's complexity. Use graphics settings that can be adjusted to maintain performance on older devices.

- **Battery Life:** Minimize the game's impact on device battery life by optimizing resource usage and avoiding unnecessary background processes.

3. User Interface (UI) Design

- **Responsive UI:** Create a responsive user interface that adapts to different screen sizes and orientations. Ensure that UI elements remain readable and usable on both portrait and landscape orientations.

- **Scaling Text and Icons:** Use scalable fonts and icons to prevent them from becoming too small or too large on different screens. Test font sizes to guarantee readability.

- **Touch Targets:** Make sure that buttons and interactive elements have adequate spacing to prevent accidental taps. Account for variations in touch accuracy on different devices.

4. Loading and Performance

- **Loading Screens:** Implement loading screens or animations to mask loading times, providing a smoother experience for players. Use efficient asset loading techniques.

- **Memory Management:** Be mindful of memory usage and avoid memory leaks. Test your game on devices with lower RAM to ensure it runs without crashing.

5. Offline Play

- **Offline Modes:** Consider adding offline gameplay modes or features that don't require a constant internet connection. This can enhance the user experience, especially in areas with unreliable connectivity.

- **Data Synchronization:** Implement mechanisms to sync game progress and data when the device reconnects to the internet after being offline.

6. Cross-Platform Compatibility

- **Android and iOS:** Test your game on both Android and iOS devices to ensure compatibility with the two major mobile platforms. Address platform-specific issues and requirements.

7. Localization and Internationalization

- **Text Handling:** Ensure that your game can handle different languages and character sets gracefully. Provide translations for text-based elements.

- **Cultural Sensitivity:** Be aware of cultural differences and sensitivities when designing gameplay, characters, and narrative elements.

8. Continuous Testing

- **Beta Testing:** Conduct beta testing on a variety of devices to identify and resolve compatibility issues, bugs, and performance bottlenecks specific to certain devices.

- **User Feedback:** Encourage players to provide feedback on their experiences with different devices. Use their input to make improvements.

Responsive design and mobile optimization are ongoing processes that require thorough testing and iteration. By prioritizing the user experience on a wide range of mobile devices, you can attract and retain a larger audience for your mobile game.

10.4. Accessing Device Features (Accelerometer, GPS)

One of the advantages of mobile game development is the ability to leverage built-in device features to enhance gameplay. In this section, we will explore how to access and utilize the device's accelerometer and GPS functionalities to create unique and interactive experiences in your mobile games.

1. Accelerometer Integration

Accelerometer Basics

The accelerometer is a sensor that measures the device's acceleration along different axes (typically X, Y, and Z). By interpreting these measurements, you can detect various device movements, such as tilting, shaking, or rotating.

Use Cases

- **Tilt Controls:** Implement tilt-based controls for character movement, steering, or object manipulation. For example, in a racing game, players can tilt the device to steer their vehicle.

- **Gestures:** Recognize specific gestures like shaking the device to trigger in-game actions, such as reloading a weapon or activating a power-up.

Code Example (JavaScript):

```javascript
// Add an event listener for device motion
window.addEventListener('devicemotion', handleMotion);

function handleMotion(event) {
  // Access acceleration data
  const acceleration = event.accelerationIncludingGravity;

  // Use acceleration values to control gameplay
  const tiltX = acceleration.x;
  const tiltY = acceleration.y;

  // Implement game logic based on tilt
  // ...
}
```

2. GPS and Location Services

GPS Integration

Accessing the device's GPS allows you to determine the player's real-world location. This feature can be used for location-based games, augmented reality (AR) experiences, and more.

Use Cases

- **Geolocation-Based Gameplay:** Create games where the player's physical location affects in-game elements. For instance, in a treasure hunt game, you can place virtual treasures in real-world locations.

- **AR Applications:** Combine GPS data with AR features to superimpose virtual objects or characters onto the real environment, creating immersive experiences.

Code Example (JavaScript):

```javascript
// Check for Geolocation support
if ("geolocation" in navigator) {
  // Get the user's current position
  navigator.geolocation.getCurrentPosition(handlePosition);
} else {
  console.error("Geolocation not supported.");
}

function handlePosition(position) {
  const latitude = position.coords.latitude;
  const longitude = position.coords.longitude;

  // Use latitude and longitude to create location-based gameplay
```

```
    // . . .
}
```

3. Permissions and Privacy

When accessing device features like the accelerometer and GPS, it's crucial to request the necessary permissions from the user. Respect user privacy and provide clear explanations of why you need access to these features. Additionally, be mindful of collecting location data and ensure it is used responsibly and in compliance with privacy regulations.

Incorporating accelerometer and GPS functionalities into your mobile games can significantly enhance user engagement and provide unique gameplay experiences. However, it's essential to strike a balance between creativity and privacy considerations when implementing these features.

10.5. Publishing and Monetizing Mobile Games

Publishing and monetizing your mobile games are crucial steps in turning your game development efforts into a successful venture. In this section, we'll explore various strategies for getting your game out to the public and generating revenue from your creations.

1. Choosing the Right Platform

Before you can publish your mobile game, you need to decide which platform(s) to target. The two primary platforms for mobile games are:

- **App Stores:** The Apple App Store for iOS devices and Google Play Store for Android devices are the most popular platforms. Publishing on these stores provides access to a vast user base.

- **Alternative Markets:** In addition to the major app stores, consider other markets, such as Amazon Appstore or Samsung Galaxy Store. These platforms may have less competition, offering more visibility for your game.

2. App Store Guidelines

Each app store has its set of guidelines and policies for app submissions. Ensure your game complies with these guidelines to avoid rejection. Common reasons for rejection include:

- **Copyright Violations:** Using copyrighted content without permission can lead to rejection. Ensure you have the rights to all assets used in your game.

- **Inappropriate Content:** Games with explicit or offensive content may be rejected. Keep your game suitable for a wide audience.

- **Privacy and Permissions:** Be transparent about the data your app collects and why it's collected. Request user permissions only when necessary.

3. Monetization Strategies

There are several ways to monetize your mobile game:

- **In-App Ads:** Display advertisements within your game. Options include banner ads, interstitials, and rewarded video ads. Ad networks like AdMob and Facebook Audience Network can help you implement ads.

- **In-App Purchases (IAPs):** Offer virtual items, power-ups, or currency for purchase within the game. IAPs can enhance gameplay and generate revenue.

- **Subscriptions:** Create subscription-based models for access to premium features or content. This works well for apps with regular updates and ongoing value.

- **Premium/Paid Apps:** Charge users an upfront fee to download and play your game. Ensure your game provides substantial value to justify the cost.

4. User Acquisition and Marketing

Getting your game noticed requires effective marketing strategies:

- **App Store Optimization (ASO):** Optimize your game's title, description, and keywords to improve visibility in app stores.

- **Social Media:** Utilize platforms like Twitter, Facebook, and Instagram to create a presence for your game and engage with potential players.

- **Press Releases:** Reach out to gaming news websites and influencers for reviews and coverage.

- **Community Building:** Create a community around your game through forums, social media groups, and Discord channels.

5. Analytics and Iteration

Track user behavior and engagement using analytics tools. Analyze player data to identify areas for improvement and iterate on your game. Understanding player preferences and habits can lead to more successful updates and monetization strategies.

6. Feedback and Support

Encourage player feedback and provide excellent customer support. Address bug reports and concerns promptly to maintain a positive reputation among your player base.

Publishing and monetizing mobile games is an ongoing process. Continuously update and improve your game, respond to user feedback, and explore new monetization opportunities to maximize your game's success in the competitive mobile gaming market.

Chapter 11: Game Testing and Debugging

Section 11.1: Fundamentals of Game Testing

Game testing is an essential phase in the game development process. It involves systematically evaluating and verifying various aspects of your game to ensure it functions as intended, is free from critical bugs, and provides an enjoyable user experience. Testing helps identify and fix issues before the game reaches players, preventing negative reviews and preserving your game's reputation. In this section, we will delve into the fundamentals of game testing, outlining its key concepts, strategies, and best practices.

The Testing Lifecycle

Game testing typically follows a structured lifecycle that can be adapted to your development process. This lifecycle involves the following stages:

1. **Test Planning:** At the outset, create a test plan that defines the scope, objectives, and testing strategy for your game. Identify the target platforms and devices, testing environments, and testing resources required.

2. **Test Design:** Develop test cases and test scripts based on your game's design and functionality. These test cases should cover various gameplay scenarios, including normal gameplay, edge cases, and error conditions.

3. **Test Execution:** Execute the test cases on different platforms, browsers, or devices, depending on your game's target audience. Record test results, including any defects or issues encountered.

4. **Defect Reporting:** When issues are identified during testing, document them in a defect tracking system. Include detailed information about the problem, steps to reproduce it, and its severity.

5. **Regression Testing:** After fixing reported defects, perform regression testing to ensure that the changes did not introduce new issues and that existing functionality still works correctly.

6. **User Acceptance Testing (UAT):** In some cases, involve external testers or even players to perform UAT to gather feedback on the overall gaming experience.

7. **Performance Testing:** Assess the game's performance, including factors like frame rate, loading times, and resource utilization. Identify and resolve performance bottlenecks.

8. **Compatibility Testing:** Ensure that the game works correctly on different devices, screen resolutions, and web browsers, addressing any compatibility issues.

9. **Security Testing:** Verify that your game is secure against common vulnerabilities such as cheating, data breaches, or unauthorized access.

Types of Game Testing

There are several types of game testing, each serving a specific purpose:

- **Functional Testing:** Focuses on testing individual functions or features of the game to ensure they work as intended.

- **Integration Testing:** Tests the interaction between different components or systems within the game to ensure they integrate smoothly.

- **Load Testing:** Evaluates the game's performance under heavy loads to identify bottlenecks and scalability issues.

- **Usability Testing:** Assesses the game's user interface, controls, and overall user experience.

- **Compatibility Testing:** Ensures the game runs on various devices, platforms, and browsers without issues.

- **Regression Testing:** Repeatedly tests previously working features after changes to catch unintended side effects.

- **Alpha Testing:** Conducted by the development team to identify and fix major issues before a wider beta test.

- **Beta Testing:** Involves external testers or players who provide feedback on the game's overall experience.

Automated Testing

Automated testing can greatly enhance the efficiency and accuracy of game testing. You can use testing frameworks and scripts to automate repetitive and time-consuming test cases. For web-based games, tools like Selenium WebDriver can be employed for automated testing on different browsers.

Continuous Integration

Integrating testing into your development pipeline through continuous integration (CI) practices ensures that tests are executed automatically whenever changes are made to the game's codebase. CI tools like Jenkins or Travis CI can be configured to run tests and report results, helping maintain code quality.

Conclusion

In this section, we've explored the fundamentals of game testing, including its lifecycle, types, and the benefits of automation and continuous integration. Effective testing is crucial to delivering a polished and bug-free game to your players, ultimately leading to a better gaming experience and improved player retention. As you progress in your game development journey, consider implementing robust testing processes to ensure the success of your games.

Section 11.2: Debugging Techniques in JavaScript

Debugging is an essential skill for game developers, as it allows you to identify and fix issues in your code effectively. JavaScript provides various debugging tools and techniques to help you track down and resolve bugs. In this section, we'll explore debugging techniques specific to JavaScript game development.

1. Browser Developer Tools:

Modern web browsers come with built-in developer tools that include powerful debugging capabilities. You can open these tools by pressing F12 or Ctrl + Shift + I (Windows/Linux) or Cmd + Option + I (Mac) while your game is running in the browser.

- **Console:** The console is the most frequently used tool for debugging JavaScript. You can use console.log(), console.error(), and console.warn() to log messages and variables' values, helping you understand what's happening in your code.

- **Debugger:** The debugger allows you to set breakpoints in your code. When execution reaches a breakpoint, it pauses, allowing you to inspect variables, step through code, and track the flow of your program.

- **Network Tab:** Use the Network tab to monitor network requests and responses, which can be helpful if your game interacts with a server or loads external assets.

2. Source Maps:

Source maps are files that map your minified or transpiled code back to its original source code. They are particularly useful when your game code has been minified or bundled. By enabling source maps in your development environment, you can debug the original code even if it's not what's running in the browser.

3. Chrome DevTools Tips:

If you're using Google Chrome, DevTools offers additional features:

- **Blackboxing:** You can "blackbox" certain scripts, telling the debugger to ignore them. This is useful when working with third-party libraries or frameworks that you don't need to debug.

- **XHR Breakpoints:** If your game uses AJAX requests, you can set XHR breakpoints to pause execution when specific XMLHttpRequests are made.

4. Logging and Assertion Libraries:

Consider using libraries like debug.js or assertion libraries like assert.js to simplify and enhance your debugging process. These libraries provide structured ways to log messages and assert conditions in your code.

5. Linters:

Linters like ESLint can help you catch common coding mistakes and enforce coding standards, which can prevent many bugs from occurring in the first place. They can also be configured to highlight potential issues directly in your code editor.

6. Unit Testing:

Unit testing frameworks like Mocha, Chai, or Jasmine allow you to write automated tests for individual parts of your code. This can help you catch bugs early and ensure that new code changes don't introduce regressions.

7. Remote Debugging:

For games running on mobile devices or other platforms, you can use remote debugging tools provided by browsers like Chrome and Firefox. These tools allow you to connect your development machine to the device and debug JavaScript code remotely.

8. Profiling:

Profiling tools can help you identify performance bottlenecks in your game. Tools like the Chrome Performance tab or the JavaScript Profiler in Firefox can show you where your code spends the most time, allowing you to optimize critical sections.

9. Memory Leak Detection:

Memory leaks can be particularly challenging to debug. Browser developer tools often include memory profiling capabilities that can help you identify and fix memory leaks in your game.

10. Error Tracking Services:

Consider integrating error tracking services like Sentry or Rollbar into your game. These services can capture and report errors that occur in the production environment, helping you fix issues reported by players.

In conclusion, debugging is an essential part of JavaScript game development. Familiarize yourself with the debugging tools provided by your browser, use source maps to debug minified code, and consider additional tools and techniques like linters, unit testing, and profiling to ensure your game code is robust and bug-free. Debugging is a skill that improves with practice, so don't hesitate to dive into your code and solve those bugs!

Section 11.3: Performance Testing and Optimization

Performance optimization is a crucial aspect of JavaScript game development. Ensuring that your game runs smoothly and efficiently can lead to a better player experience. In this section, we'll explore performance testing and optimization techniques specific to JavaScript games.

1. Profiling Your Game:

Profiling is the process of measuring the performance of your game to identify bottlenecks and areas for improvement. Modern web browsers offer built-in profiling tools that allow you to analyze CPU usage, memory consumption, and other performance metrics.

- **CPU Profiling:** Use the CPU profiler in browser developer tools to identify which functions or code blocks are consuming the most CPU resources. Look for performance-critical areas that might benefit from optimization.

- **Memory Profiling:** Memory profiling tools can help you detect memory leaks and unnecessary memory consumption. Analyze memory snapshots to identify objects that are not being properly garbage collected.

2. Frame Rate Optimization:

Maintaining a consistent frame rate is essential for a smooth gaming experience. Here are some tips for optimizing frame rate:

- **Use RequestAnimationFrame:** Instead of using `setInterval` or `setTimeout` for animation loops, use `requestAnimationFrame`, which is designed for smooth animations and automatically adjusts to the user's display refresh rate.

- **Minimize Repaints:** Reduce unnecessary repaints and reflows by minimizing DOM manipulation during gameplay. Use CSS transforms and opacity changes for animations whenever possible.

- **Texture Atlases:** Combine small images into texture atlases to reduce the number of texture swaps during rendering. This can significantly improve rendering performance, especially for 2D games.

- **Culling:** Implement object culling to avoid rendering off-screen objects. This reduces the number of draw calls and improves rendering performance.

3. Optimizing JavaScript Code:

Optimizing your JavaScript code can lead to significant performance improvements:

- **Minify and Bundle:** Minify your JavaScript code to reduce file size and use bundlers like Webpack to bundle multiple scripts into a single file. Smaller files load faster.

- **Avoid Global Variables:** Minimize the use of global variables, as they can negatively impact performance. Use module patterns or ES6 modules to encapsulate code.

- **Reduce DOM Manipulation:** Minimize direct DOM manipulation. Cache references to DOM elements and manipulate them in memory before updating the actual DOM. This reduces layout thrashing.

- **Debounce and Throttle:** When handling events like window resizing or scrolling, use debounce and throttle techniques to limit the frequency of function calls and avoid excessive computation.

4. Memory Management:

Efficient memory management is crucial for preventing memory leaks and maintaining stable performance:

- **Garbage Collection:** Understand how JavaScript garbage collection works and ensure that objects are properly dereferenced when they are no longer needed.

- **Object Pooling:** Implement object pooling for frequently created and destroyed objects, such as projectiles or particles. Reusing objects instead of creating new ones can reduce memory allocation overhead.

- **Dispose of Resources:** Release resources like event listeners, timers, and web workers when they are no longer needed. Failing to do so can lead to memory leaks.

5. Network Optimization:

If your game involves network requests, consider these optimization techniques:

- **Minimize HTTP Requests:** Reduce the number of HTTP requests by bundling assets, using spritesheets, and lazy loading resources as needed.

- **Content Delivery Networks (CDNs):** Use CDNs to deliver assets closer to the player, reducing latency and loading times.

- **Compression:** Compress assets like images, audio, and JSON data to reduce download times.

- **Caching:** Implement client-side caching strategies to store frequently used assets locally, reducing the need for re-downloading.

6. Browser Compatibility:

Ensure that your game is optimized for various web browsers and devices. Test your game on multiple browsers and use feature detection to provide fallbacks for unsupported features.

In conclusion, optimizing the performance of your JavaScript game is essential for delivering a smooth and enjoyable player experience. Use profiling tools to identify performance bottlenecks, optimize your code, and implement best practices for rendering, memory management, and network optimization. Regular performance testing and optimization should be an ongoing part of your game development process to ensure that your game runs efficiently on a wide range of devices and platforms.

Section 11.4: Cross-Browser and Cross-Platform Testing

Cross-browser and cross-platform compatibility testing is a critical aspect of JavaScript game development. Ensuring that your game works well on different web browsers and devices is essential for reaching a broader audience and providing a consistent player experience. In this section, we'll explore techniques and best practices for cross-browser and cross-platform testing.

1. Browser Compatibility:

JavaScript games can behave differently across various web browsers due to differences in JavaScript engines and HTML/CSS rendering. Here are some tips for testing browser compatibility:

- **Use Browser Developer Tools:** Each major browser offers developer tools that allow you to inspect and debug your game. Familiarize yourself with these tools to identify and resolve browser-specific issues.

- **Test on Multiple Browsers:** Test your game on popular web browsers like Chrome, Firefox, Safari, Edge, and Internet Explorer (if still relevant). Consider using browser testing services that provide virtual environments for testing different browser versions.

- **Feature Detection:** Instead of browser detection, use feature detection to check if a specific JavaScript or CSS feature is supported. Libraries like Modernizr can help with feature detection.

- **Polyfills:** If your game relies on modern JavaScript features, consider using polyfills to provide support for older browsers. Polyfills add missing functionality to older browsers.

2. Responsive Design:

Games should adapt to different screen sizes and orientations. Responsive design is essential for cross-platform compatibility:

- **Media Queries:** Use CSS media queries to create responsive layouts that adjust based on the screen size. Ensure that your game's UI elements are appropriately scaled and positioned for different devices.

- **Touch and Mouse Events:** Test both touch and mouse interactions to accommodate users on touchscreen devices and traditional computers.

- **Mobile Emulators:** Utilize mobile emulators or device testing labs to test your game on a variety of mobile devices and screen sizes.

Performance can vary significantly between devices and platforms. To ensure a consistent gaming experience, perform performance testing on a range of devices:

- **Device Testing:** Test your game on different smartphones, tablets, and desktop computers. Pay attention to performance on lower-end devices, as they may have limited processing power and memory.

- **Performance Metrics:** Use performance profiling tools to measure frame rate, CPU usage, and memory consumption on various devices. Address performance issues to provide a smooth gaming experience.

4. Input Methods:

Consider the various input methods used by players on different platforms:

- **Keyboard and Mouse:** Ensure that your game's controls and UI elements work seamlessly with keyboard and mouse inputs on desktop platforms.

- **Touchscreen:** Optimize touch controls and gestures for mobile devices and tablets. Test swipe, tap, and pinch gestures for responsiveness and accuracy.

- **Game Controllers:** If your game supports game controllers, test compatibility with popular controllers like Xbox and PlayStation controllers.

5. Cross-Platform Libraries and Frameworks:

When building cross-platform games, consider using libraries and frameworks that provide cross-platform compatibility out of the box. Examples include Phaser, Three.js, and Unity WebGL export for web games.

6. User Testing:

Conduct user testing with players on different devices and platforms to gather feedback and identify issues. User testing can provide valuable insights into how players interact with your game and any usability issues they encounter.

In summary, cross-browser and cross-platform testing is essential to ensure that your JavaScript game functions correctly and performs well across a wide range of web browsers and devices. Use developer tools, responsive design techniques, and performance testing to address compatibility issues. Regular testing and user feedback will help you deliver a consistent and enjoyable gaming experience to players regardless of their choice of device or browser.

Section 11.5: User Testing and Feedback Integration

User testing is a critical phase in the game development process that helps you gather valuable feedback, identify issues, and refine your game. This section explores the importance of user testing and how to effectively integrate user feedback into your JavaScript game development workflow.

1. The Importance of User Testing:

User testing involves real players interacting with your game, providing insights into their experiences. Here's why it's essential:

- **Identify Usability Issues:** User testing helps uncover usability issues, such as confusing controls, unclear instructions, or frustrating gameplay elements.

- **Detect Bugs and Glitches:** Players can find bugs and glitches that you might have missed during development, helping you improve game stability.

- **Evaluate Game Balance:** User testing helps evaluate game balance, ensuring that the difficulty level is appropriate and that players find the game enjoyable.

- **Gather Feedback:** It provides valuable feedback from the target audience, helping you make informed decisions about game design and features.

2. Planning User Testing:

Before conducting user testing, it's crucial to plan the process:

- **Define Objectives:** Clearly outline the goals and objectives of your user testing. What specific aspects of the game do you want to evaluate?

- **Select Testers:** Choose a diverse group of testers representing your target audience. This can include players of different skill levels and backgrounds.

- **Create Test Scenarios:** Develop test scenarios or tasks that testers should complete while playing the game. These scenarios should align with your testing objectives.

- **Prepare Testing Environment:** Set up a controlled testing environment with the necessary equipment and software for recording gameplay and capturing user feedback.

3. Conducting User Testing:

During user testing, follow these guidelines:

- **Observe and Record:** Have testers play your game while you observe their actions and reactions. Record video and audio to capture their interactions and comments.

- **Ask Questions:** Encourage testers to share their thoughts, feelings, and feedback while playing. Ask open-ended questions to gather insights.

- **Minimize Interruptions:** Minimize interruptions and distractions during testing to obtain authentic feedback.

- **Collect Data:** Collect quantitative data, such as completion times or success rates, and qualitative data, including user comments and observations.

- **Iterate and Refine:** Use the feedback from user testing to make iterative improvements to your game. Prioritize issues and address critical issues first.

4. Feedback Integration:

Once you have gathered feedback, it's essential to integrate it into your development process:

- **Prioritize Feedback:** Sort feedback into categories, such as critical, important, and nice-to-have. Address critical issues first to improve the overall game experience.

- **Iterate on Design:** Make design changes based on user feedback, whether it involves adjusting gameplay mechanics, enhancing graphics, or refining user interfaces.

- **Bug Fixing:** Address reported bugs and glitches promptly. Test the fixes thoroughly to ensure they resolve the issues.

- **Game Balancing:** Use feedback to fine-tune game balance, making adjustments to difficulty levels, enemy behavior, or resource distribution.

- **Usability Improvements:** Implement usability improvements based on user suggestions, such as clarifying instructions or simplifying controls.

5. Continuous Testing:

User testing isn't a one-time event. It should be an ongoing process throughout development. Regularly test new features, updates, and gameplay improvements with user feedback in mind.

6. Usability Testing Tools:

Consider using usability testing tools and platforms that facilitate remote testing and provide insights into player behavior and feedback. Tools like UserTesting.com or PlaytestCloud can be valuable resources.

In conclusion, user testing and feedback integration are essential steps in the JavaScript game development process. By involving real players and gathering their insights, you can create a more enjoyable and polished gaming experience. Use this feedback to iteratively improve your game, addressing issues, and refining your design until you achieve a product that resonates with your target audience.

144

Chapter 12: Game Analytics and Player Engagement

Section 12.1: Integrating Analytics Tools

Game analytics is a crucial aspect of modern game development. It involves the collection and analysis of player data to understand player behavior, preferences, and engagement levels. This data-driven approach helps developers make informed decisions, improve game design, and enhance player engagement. In this section, we'll explore the integration of analytics tools into your JavaScript games.

1. Why Use Analytics:

Game analytics provides several benefits:

- **Player Understanding:** Analytics tools help you gain insights into how players interact with your game. You can see which features they use, how long they play, and where they might drop off.

- **Iterative Improvement:** By analyzing player data, you can make data-driven decisions to iterate and improve your game. This leads to better player experiences.

- **Player Retention:** Understanding player behavior can help you implement strategies to retain players, reducing churn.

- **Monetization Optimization:** For games with in-app purchases or ads, analytics can help optimize revenue generation by identifying which monetization strategies work best.

2. Choosing an Analytics Tool:

There are various analytics tools available, both free and paid. Some popular choices for JavaScript game development include:

- **Google Analytics:** Widely used for web-based games, it provides extensive tracking capabilities and integrates well with web development.

- **Unity Analytics:** If you're developing games using the Unity game engine, Unity Analytics is a seamless choice.

- **Mixpanel:** Offers a user-friendly interface and powerful event tracking for in-depth analysis.

- **Amplitude:** Known for its user behavior analytics and retention analysis features.

- **Custom Solutions:** For more advanced needs, you can build your custom analytics system tailored to your game.

3. Instrumentation and Event Tracking:

To use analytics effectively, you need to instrument your game by adding tracking code and defining events to monitor. Events are specific player actions or interactions you want to track. For example:

- Tracking game starts, level completions, or tutorial steps.
- Monitoring in-game purchases, ad views, or social interactions.
- Recording player deaths, achievements, or high scores.

4. Data Privacy and Compliance:

When collecting player data, it's crucial to respect privacy and comply with relevant regulations like GDPR or COPPA. Always provide clear privacy policies and obtain user consent for data collection when necessary.

5. Analyzing and Acting on Data:

Once you start collecting data, it's time to analyze it. Analytics tools provide dashboards and reports that help you interpret the data. Here's what you can do with the insights:

- **Identify Pain Points:** Look for patterns in player behavior to find pain points or areas of improvement.

- **A/B Testing:** Experiment with different game features or monetization strategies and use analytics to compare results.

- **Player Segmentation:** Segment players based on behavior and tailor experiences or offers accordingly.

- **Predictive Analytics:** Use historical data to predict future player behavior and adapt your game accordingly.

- **Engagement Strategies:** Create engagement strategies based on player preferences, such as sending personalized notifications or rewards.

- **Retention Tactics:** Implement retention tactics to keep players coming back, like daily rewards or events.

6. Continuous Analysis and Improvement:

Analytics is an ongoing process. Regularly analyze data and use it to inform updates and improvements to your game. As player behavior evolves, so should your game.

In summary, integrating analytics tools into your JavaScript game development process is essential for understanding player behavior and enhancing player engagement. By choosing the right analytics tool, instrumenting your game effectively, respecting data privacy, and continuously analyzing and acting on data, you can create a more successful and engaging gaming experience for your players.

Section 12.2: Tracking Player Behavior and Preferences

Once you've integrated analytics tools into your JavaScript game, the next step is to track player behavior and preferences. This involves collecting and analyzing data on how players interact with your game, what they enjoy, and what might need improvement. In this section, we'll explore how to effectively track player behavior and preferences to improve your game.

1. Defining Key Metrics:

To track player behavior and preferences, you need to define key metrics or events that are relevant to your game. These metrics will help you understand how players engage with your game. Common key metrics include:

- **Retention Rate:** How many players return to your game over time.
- **Session Length:** The average duration of a gaming session.
- **In-App Purchases:** Tracking revenue generated from in-game purchases.
- **Level Completion:** Monitoring progress through your game's levels.
- **User Acquisition:** How players find and install your game.

2. Event Tracking:

To collect data on these metrics, you'll need to implement event tracking in your game. Events are specific actions or interactions within the game that you want to monitor. For example:

- Tracking when a player completes a level.
- Recording when a player makes an in-app purchase.
- Monitoring how often players watch ads for in-game rewards.

Here's an example of how event tracking can be implemented in JavaScript:

```javascript
// Track when a level is completed
function trackLevelCompletion(levelNumber) {
  // Send an event to your analytics tool
  analytics.track('Level Completed', {
    level: levelNumber,
    playerID: currentPlayerID,
  });
}

// Track in-app purchase
function trackInAppPurchase(productID, amount) {
  // Send an event to your analytics tool
  analytics.track('In-App Purchase', {
```

```
    product: productID,
    amount: amount,
    playerID: currentPlayerID,
  });
}
```

3. Player Preferences:

Understanding player preferences is equally important. To track player preferences, consider the following:

- **Player Surveys:** Conduct player surveys or feedback forms within your game to gather direct input from players.

- **Heatmaps:** Use heatmap tools to visualize where players click, interact, or spend the most time in your game.

- **A/B Testing:** Experiment with different game mechanics, features, or visuals to see what players respond to best.

- **Social Media Listening:** Monitor social media channels and forums to see what players are saying about your game.

4. Analytics Dashboards:

Most analytics tools provide dashboards that display data in a user-friendly manner. These dashboards help you visualize player behavior and preferences over time. Regularly review these dashboards to identify trends or anomalies.

5. Iterative Game Development:

Tracking player behavior and preferences should lead to iterative game development. Based on the data collected, make informed decisions about game updates and improvements. For example:

- If players are struggling with a particular level, consider adjusting its difficulty.
- If in-app purchases are low, reevaluate your monetization strategy.
- If players love a specific feature, expand on it or create more similar content.

6. Privacy and Data Security:

When collecting player data, prioritize privacy and data security. Ensure you have clear privacy policies, and only collect data that is necessary for improving the player's gaming experience. Always obtain user consent when required by regulations.

In conclusion, tracking player behavior and preferences is essential for creating engaging and successful JavaScript games. Define key metrics, implement event tracking, and use analytics dashboards to gather insights. Regularly analyze data, make informed decisions, and iterate on your game to improve player satisfaction and retention.

Section 12.3: Using Data for Game Improvements

Once you've gathered data on player behavior and preferences in your JavaScript game, it's time to put that data to use for game improvements. In this section, we'll explore how you can leverage the insights gained from analytics to enhance your game.

1. Identifying Problem Areas:

Start by identifying areas of your game that need improvement. Analyze the data collected to pinpoint specific issues. For example:

- If the retention rate drops after a certain level, that level might be too difficult.
- If players frequently abandon the game during onboarding, consider improving the tutorial.
- Low in-app purchases may indicate a need for better monetization strategies.

2. Prioritizing Improvements:

Not all issues are equal, and you may have limited resources. Prioritize improvements based on their potential impact on player satisfaction and game success. Consider factors like:

- The severity of the issue.
- The number of players affected.
- The potential increase in player retention or revenue.

3. Iterative Development:

Take an iterative approach to game development. Instead of making sweeping changes, implement small, targeted improvements, and monitor their impact. This allows you to course-correct if needed and avoid introducing new issues.

4. User Feedback:

Combine data-driven insights with user feedback. Encourage players to provide feedback within the game or through other channels. This qualitative input can offer valuable context and help you understand the "why" behind certain behaviors.

5. Testing and Validation:

Before implementing significant changes, conduct testing and validation. Create prototypes or beta versions to test new features or adjustments. Collect feedback from a smaller group of players to identify any unforeseen issues.

6. Monetization Optimization:

For monetization-focused improvements, analyze data related to in-app purchases and ad revenue. Experiment with different monetization models, pricing strategies, and ad implementations to find what resonates best with your audience.

7. Performance Optimization:

Performance issues, such as slow load times or crashes, can lead to player frustration. Use performance data to identify bottlenecks and areas for optimization. Ensure your game runs smoothly across various devices and browsers.

8. Content Updates:

Regularly update your game with new content, features, or challenges. Analyze data on player engagement to determine which types of content are most popular and use this information to inform your updates.

9. Community Engagement:

Engage with your player community and use their feedback to shape improvements. Hosting events, forums, or social media discussions can provide insights and create a sense of community around your game.

10. Analytics Tools:

Continuously monitor player behavior and preferences using analytics tools. As your game evolves, the data you collect will change, so adapt your tracking accordingly.

11. Privacy and Data Ethics:

Always handle player data ethically and in compliance with relevant regulations. Be transparent about the data you collect and how it's used. Protect player privacy and ensure their trust in your game.

In conclusion, using data for game improvements is a crucial part of the game development process. By analyzing player behavior and preferences, identifying issues, and making targeted improvements, you can create a more engaging and successful JavaScript game. Remember to take an iterative approach, prioritize wisely, and maintain a strong focus on player satisfaction.

Section 12.4: Engagement Strategies and Retention Techniques

Engagement and player retention are critical factors for the success of your JavaScript game. In this section, we'll delve into strategies and techniques to keep players engaged and coming back for more.

1. Regular Content Updates:

One effective way to maintain player interest is by regularly updating your game with new content. This can include new levels, characters, challenges, or events. Frequent updates provide players with fresh experiences and reasons to return.

2. Events and Challenges:

Hosting in-game events and challenges adds excitement and variety to your game. These time-limited activities can offer exclusive rewards, fostering a sense of urgency and encouraging players to log in regularly.

```
// Example of an in-game event countdown
const eventEndTime = new Date('2024-01-31T18:00:00').getTime();

function updateEventCountdown() {
  const now = new Date().getTime();
  const timeRemaining = eventEndTime - now;

  // Update the UI with the time remaining
  // ...

  if (timeRemaining <= 0) {
    // Event has ended, remove it from the game
    // ...
  }
}

setInterval(updateEventCountdown, 1000);
```

3. Daily Rewards:

Implement a daily rewards system to incentivize daily logins. Offer bonuses, such as in-game currency, items, or experience points, for consecutive logins. This habit-forming mechanic can help boost retention.

```
// Example of a daily rewards system
let consecutiveLogins = 0;

function claimDailyReward() {
  if (hasPlayerLoggedInToday()) {
    consecutiveLogins++;
    grantReward(consecutiveLogins);
  } else {
    consecutiveLogins = 0;
  }
}
```

4. Social Features:

Incorporate social features that allow players to connect and interact with friends or other players. Features like in-game chat, friend lists, and multiplayer modes can enhance the social aspect of your game.

5. Achievements and Progression:

Implement achievement systems and progression mechanics. Recognize and reward player accomplishments with badges, trophies, or in-game titles. Clearly define goals and provide a sense of accomplishment as players advance.

```
// Example of unlocking an achievement
function unlockAchievement(player, achievement) {
  if (!player.hasAchievement(achievement)) {
    player.addAchievement(achievement);
    player.gainExperience(achievement.rewardXP);
    notifyPlayer(`Achievement Unlocked: ${achievement.name}`);
  }
}
```

6. Personalization:

Allow players to personalize their gaming experience. Customizable avatars, character skins, or in-game homes can create a sense of ownership and attachment to the game.

```
// Example of avatar customization
function customizeAvatar(player, customizationOptions) {
  player.avatar.customize(customizationOptions);
}
```

7. Feedback and Communication:

Encourage player feedback and communication. Provide ways for players to report issues, suggest improvements, or share their experiences. Act on feedback to demonstrate that you value player input.

8. Community Building:

Foster a sense of community among players. Create forums, social media groups, or Discord channels where players can discuss the game, share tips, and connect with fellow gamers.

9. Cross-Platform Play:

If possible, enable cross-platform play so that players on different devices can interact. This broadens the player base and increases the potential for social connections.

10. Surprise and Delight:

Occasionally surprise players with unexpected content or events. These surprises can create memorable moments and generate buzz within the player community.

In conclusion, player engagement and retention are ongoing efforts in the world of JavaScript gaming. By implementing these strategies and techniques, you can create a dynamic and vibrant player community that continues to enjoy and support your game. Keep a close eye on player feedback and analytics to fine-tune your engagement strategies over time.

Section 12.5: Implementing Achievements and Rewards

Achievements and rewards are essential elements in many games that add depth, challenge, and motivation for players. In this section, we'll explore how to implement achievement systems and reward structures in JavaScript games.

1. Defining Achievements:

Before implementing achievements, you need to define them. Consider what accomplishments or milestones players can achieve in your game. Achievements can range from completing specific levels to mastering advanced skills.

```
// Example achievement definition
const achievements = [
  {
    id: 'level_completion',
    name: 'Level Completion',
    description: 'Complete the tutorial level.',
  },
  {
    id: 'high_score',
    name: 'High Score',
    description: 'Achieve a score of 10,000 or more.',
  },
  // Add more achievements...
];
```

2. Tracking Progress:

To determine whether players have earned achievements, you must track their progress. This often involves setting up event listeners and handlers to detect specific in-game actions or milestones.

```
// Example of tracking progress for level completion
function trackLevelCompletion(player, levelId) {
  // Check if the level matches the tutorial level
  if (levelId === 'tutorial') {
    // Update the player's progress for the 'level_completion' achievement
    player.updateAchievementProgress('level_completion', 1);
```

```
    }
}
```

3. Unlocking Achievements:

When players meet the criteria for an achievement, you should unlock it and notify the player. Ensure that achievements are stored and associated with each player's profile.

```
// Example of unlocking an achievement
function unlockAchievement(player, achievementId) {
  if (!player.hasAchievement(achievementId)) {
    player.addAchievement(achievementId);
    notifyPlayer(`Achievement Unlocked: ${getAchievementName(achievementId)}`
);
  }
}
```

4. Rewarding Players:

Achievements often come with rewards, which can include in-game currency, items, or experience points. Rewards serve as incentives for players to pursue and complete achievements.

```
// Example of rewarding players for achievements
function rewardPlayerForAchievement(player, achievementId) {
  const achievement = getAchievementById(achievementId);
  if (achievement) {
    player.gainRewards(achievement.rewards);
  }
}
```

5. Displaying Achievements:

Create a user-friendly interface where players can view their achievements and progress. This can be a dedicated achievements screen or an overlay that appears during gameplay.

```
// Example of displaying achievements to the player
function displayAchievements(player) {
  const playerAchievements = player.getAchievements();
  // Render the list of achievements in the UI
  // ...
}
```

6. Challenging Achievements:

Include a mix of easy, moderate, and challenging achievements to cater to different player skill levels. Challenging achievements can be rare and prestigious, while easy ones offer a sense of progression.

```
// Example of a challenging achievement
const achievements = [
  {
```

```
    id: 'easy_completion',
    name: 'Easy Completion',
    description: 'Complete any level.',
  },
  {
    id: 'moderate_completion',
    name: 'Moderate Completion',
    description: 'Complete all levels in medium difficulty.',
  },
  {
    id: 'hard_completion',
    name: 'Hard Completion',
    description: 'Complete all levels in hard difficulty.',
  },
];
```

7. Player Profile and Persistence:

Ensure that player achievements and progress are persistent across gaming sessions. Store this data either on the server or locally on the player's device, depending on the game's architecture.

```
// Example of saving player progress and achievements
function savePlayerData(player) {
  // Store player achievements and progress
  // ...
}
```

8. Feedback and Celebration:

Celebrate achievements with animations, sound effects, or pop-up notifications to make players feel accomplished. Positive feedback enhances the player's experience.

```
// Example of displaying a celebration animation
function celebrateAchievement() {
  // Play a confetti animation
  // Show a "Congratulations!" message
  // Play a fanfare sound effect
}
```

Incorporating achievements and rewards into your JavaScript game can significantly enhance player engagement and retention. By carefully designing achievements and their associated rewards, you can motivate players to explore your game thoroughly and set new goals for themselves. Keep in mind that the balance of difficulty and the uniqueness of achievements can greatly impact the player's experience, so continually iterate and refine your achievement system based on player feedback.

Chapter 13: Advanced Game Mechanics

Section 13.1: Implementing Complex Game Systems

In this section, we'll explore the implementation of complex game systems that can elevate your JavaScript game to the next level. These systems involve intricate rules, interactions, and mechanics that create depth and engagement for players. Implementing such systems requires careful planning and coding to ensure they function seamlessly within your game.

1. Designing Complex Game Systems:

Before diving into implementation, it's crucial to have a well-thought-out design for your complex game systems. These systems can include:

- **Quest and mission systems:** Creating a branching narrative with multiple quests and missions.
- **Economy and trading systems:** Implementing a virtual economy where players can buy, sell, and trade in-game items.
- **Skill and leveling systems:** Allowing characters or players to gain experience points, level up, and choose abilities.
- **Time and weather systems:** Simulating day-night cycles and weather conditions that affect gameplay.
- **Crafting and item customization:** Letting players craft items and customize equipment.

2. Modular Architecture:

To manage complex game systems efficiently, adopt a modular architecture for your codebase. Break down each system into smaller, reusable components or modules. This approach simplifies maintenance and allows for easy expansion.

```
// Example of modular architecture
class QuestSystem {
  // Quest-related functions and logic
}

class EconomySystem {
  // Economy-related functions and logic
}

class LevelingSystem {
  // Leveling-related functions and logic
}
```

3. Data-Driven Design:

Store game system data in external files or databases to enable easy modifications and tuning without changing the code. Use formats like JSON or XML to define quests, items, skills, and other game elements.

```
// Example JSON data for quests
{
  "quests": [
    {
      "id": "quest001",
      "name": "Rescue the Villagers",
      "description": "Save the villagers from a dragon attack.",
      "reward": {
        "experience": 100,
        "gold": 50
      }
    },
    // More quests...
  ]
}
```

4. Event-Driven Systems:

Complex game systems often involve numerous events and interactions. Implement an event-driven architecture to handle these events efficiently. Use event listeners and emitters to manage interactions between different parts of your game.

```
// Example of event-driven system
class EventSystem {
  constructor() {
    this.listeners = {};
  }

  on(event, callback) {
    if (!this.listeners[event]) {
      this.listeners[event] = [];
    }
    this.listeners[event].push(callback);
  }

  emit(event, data) {
    if (this.listeners[event]) {
      for (const callback of this.listeners[event]) {
        callback(data);
      }
    }
  }
}
```

5. Testing and Balancing:

Complex game systems require thorough testing to ensure they function as intended. Test each system in isolation and then together to identify any conflicts or unexpected behaviors. Balance the game mechanics to provide a satisfying player experience.

6. Iterative Development:

Complex systems may not be perfect on the first attempt. Be prepared for iterative development, where you refine and improve your systems based on player feedback and analytics. Regular updates and patches can enhance the gameplay experience.

7. Documentation and Communication:

Document your complex game systems thoroughly, both for your own reference and for potential collaborators. Effective communication within your development team is crucial to ensure everyone understands the mechanics and how they interact.

Implementing complex game systems can be challenging but rewarding. These systems can set your game apart, providing depth and immersion that captivate players. However, remember that complexity should serve the player's enjoyment, so always prioritize user experience when designing and implementing these advanced game mechanics.

Section 13.2: Creating Puzzle and Strategy Elements

In this section, we'll delve into the implementation of puzzle and strategy elements in your JavaScript game. These elements can add depth, challenge, and engagement to your gameplay, making it more enjoyable for your players. Whether you're developing a puzzle-based adventure or a strategy-focused game, understanding how to create and integrate these elements is essential.

1. Designing Puzzle Elements:

Puzzle elements involve challenges that players need to solve through logic, reasoning, or creativity. They can be standalone puzzles or integrated into the storyline. When designing puzzles, consider the following:

- **Difficulty curve:** Start with easy puzzles and gradually increase complexity to keep players engaged.
- **Variety:** Include a range of puzzle types, such as riddles, mazes, and pattern recognition.
- **Feedback:** Provide clear feedback when a player completes or fails a puzzle.
- **Intuitiveness:** Ensure that puzzles are intuitive and don't require obscure solutions.

2. Implementing Puzzle Mechanics:

Implementing puzzle mechanics requires careful coding and logic. Use conditional statements, event triggers, and variables to control puzzle behavior. Here's a simplified example of a puzzle where the player needs to match symbols:

```javascript
// Example puzzle logic
const puzzleSymbols = ['A', 'B', 'C'];
let playerSelection = [];

function checkPuzzleSolution() {
  if (playerSelection.length === puzzleSymbols.length) {
    const isSolutionCorrect = playerSelection.every(
      (symbol, index) => symbol === puzzleSymbols[index]
    );

    if (isSolutionCorrect) {
      // Puzzle solved, trigger reward or progression
      console.log('Puzzle solved!');
    } else {
      // Reset player's selection
      playerSelection = [];
      console.log('Incorrect solution. Try again.');
    }
  }
}

// Player interaction
function onSymbolSelected(symbol) {
  playerSelection.push(symbol);
  checkPuzzleSolution();
}
```

3. Strategy Elements in Gameplay:

Strategy elements require players to make decisions and plan their actions strategically. They often involve resource management, tactical combat, or base-building. When incorporating strategy elements, keep these principles in mind:

- **Balancing:** Ensure that strategic decisions have meaningful consequences and that there are multiple viable strategies.
- **Depth:** Provide depth in gameplay by offering various strategies, unit types, or upgrades.
- **AI Opponents:** If your game includes AI opponents, design them to exhibit strategic behavior and challenge players.

4. Implementing Strategy Mechanics:

Implementing strategy elements involves creating game rules, handling resource allocation, and managing player choices. Here's a simplified example of a turn-based strategy game where players control armies:

```javascript
// Example strategy game mechanics
class Army {
  constructor(health, attack) {
    this.health = health;
    this.attack = attack;
  }
}

class Player {
  constructor() {
    this.army = new Army(100, 20);
    this.resources = 100;
  }

  attackEnemy(enemy) {
    enemy.health -= this.army.attack;
  }
}

class Enemy {
  constructor() {
    this.army = new Army(80, 15);
  }
}

// Player and enemy interaction
const player = new Player();
const enemy = new Enemy();

// Player's turn
player.attackEnemy(enemy);

// Enemy's turn (AI logic)
enemy.attackEnemy(player);

// Check for victory conditions
if (player.army.health <= 0) {
  console.log('You lose.');
} else if (enemy.army.health <= 0) {
  console.log('You win!');
}
```

5. Iterative Testing and Balancing:

Both puzzles and strategy elements benefit from iterative testing and balancing. Playtesters' feedback can help refine puzzles and ensure that strategic choices are meaningful and enjoyable.

6. Narrative Integration:

Consider how puzzles and strategy elements fit into your game's narrative. They can advance the storyline, unlock new areas, or reveal hidden lore. Story-driven integration can make these elements more engaging.

Incorporating puzzles and strategy elements into your JavaScript game can enhance player engagement and satisfaction. Whether you're creating brain-teasing puzzles or complex strategic decisions, a well-implemented gameplay experience can make your game memorable and enjoyable.

Section 13.3: Dynamic Storytelling and Branching Narratives

Dynamic storytelling and branching narratives are powerful techniques to engage players and provide them with a sense of agency in your JavaScript game. These storytelling methods allow players to make choices that influence the game's plot, characters, and outcomes. In this section, we'll explore how to implement dynamic storytelling and branching narratives in your game.

1. Designing Branching Narratives:

Before diving into code implementation, it's crucial to design your branching narrative. Consider the following aspects:

- **Plot Points:** Identify key decision points in your story where players' choices will matter.
- **Character Development:** Think about how character relationships and personalities evolve based on player choices.
- **Multiple Endings:** Decide if your game will have multiple endings, each influenced by different choices.
- **Consequences:** Determine the consequences of each choice, both immediate and long-term.

2. Choice Mechanism:

To implement branching narratives, you'll need a choice mechanism that allows players to make decisions. Here's a simple example of how you can create a choice system in JavaScript:

```javascript
// Example choice mechanism
const choices = [
  {
    text: 'Help the injured traveler.',
    consequences: {
      reputation: +10,
      items: ['Health Potion'],
    },
  },
  {
    text: 'Ignore the injured traveler.',
    consequences: {
      reputation: -5,
      items: [],
    },
  },
];

function presentChoices() {
  console.log('You encounter an injured traveler. What do you do?');
  choices.forEach((choice, index) => {
    console.log(`${index + 1}. ${choice.text}`);
  });
}

function handleChoice(playerChoice) {
  const selectedChoice = choices[playerChoice - 1];
  // Apply consequences based on the selected choice
  player.reputation += selectedChoice.consequences.reputation;
  player.inventory.push(...selectedChoice.consequences.items);
}
```

3. Tracking Choices and Outcomes:

To maintain a dynamic narrative, you should track players' choices and their consequences.
You can use variables, data structures, or even external files to store this information.
Ensure that the game's state reflects the choices made by the player.

```javascript
// Example choice tracking
const player = {
  reputation: 0,
  inventory: [],
};


// Player's choice
const playerChoice = 1; // Assuming the player chooses to help the injured tr
aveler

// Handle the choice and update the game state
handleChoice(playerChoice);
```

```
// Later in the game, you can reference the player's reputation or inventory
to affect the narrative.
```

4. Conditional Story Progression:

Conditional statements play a significant role in branching narratives. Use if, else if, and else statements to control the flow of the story based on the player's choices and the game's state.

```
// Example conditional story progression
if (player.reputation >= 20) {
  console.log('You have gained the trust of the local villagers.');
} else if (player.reputation >= 10) {
  console.log('The villagers are cautiously friendly toward you.');
} else {
  console.log('The villagers are wary of your presence.');
}
```

5. Testing and Iteration:

Testing is crucial to ensure that your branching narrative works as intended. Playtest your game, make different choices, and verify that the consequences align with your design. Be prepared to iterate and make adjustments to the narrative for a smoother player experience.

6. Narrative Flowcharts:

Consider creating flowcharts or diagrams to visualize your branching narrative. This can help you plan and implement the story logic effectively.

7. Performance Considerations:

Large branching narratives with numerous choices and consequences can become complex. Optimize your code and data structures to ensure smooth performance, especially if your game has extensive storytelling.

Dynamic storytelling and branching narratives can make your JavaScript game more immersive and replayable. By allowing players to shape the story through their choices, you create a deeper connection between the player and the game world. Careful design and implementation are key to a successful narrative-driven gaming experience.

Section 13.4: Economy Systems and In-Game Transactions

Economy systems and in-game transactions play a crucial role in many JavaScript games, especially in free-to-play or freemium models. These systems involve virtual currencies, items, and transactions that allow players to enhance their gaming experience. In this section, we'll explore how to implement economy systems and in-game transactions in your JavaScript game.

1. Virtual Currencies:

Virtual currencies are at the core of most in-game economies. These currencies, often represented as coins, gems, or other thematic units, can be earned through gameplay or purchased with real money. Consider the following steps to implement virtual currencies:

- **Define Currency Types:** Identify the types of virtual currencies your game will use.
- **Initial Currency Balance:** Assign an initial balance to players when they start the game.
- **Currency Earning:** Determine how players can earn currency through gameplay (e.g., completing quests, winning battles).
- **Currency Purchasing:** Implement a store where players can buy virtual currency using real money.

```javascript
// Example virtual currency implementation
const player = {
  coins: 1000,
  gems: 50,
};

// Function to purchase virtual currency
function purchaseCurrency(currencyType, amount, realMoney) {
  if (realMoney) {
    // Implement the real money transaction logic here
  } else {
    // Update the player's virtual currency balance
    player[currencyType] += amount;
  }
}
```

2. In-Game Items:

In-game items can be bought or earned using virtual currencies. These items may include power-ups, cosmetics, or equipment that enhance gameplay or customization. Consider the following when implementing in-game items:

- **Item Catalog:** Create a catalog of available items, each with a unique ID.
- **Item Attributes:** Define item attributes, such as name, description, and price in virtual currency.
- **Item Ownership:** Track which items players own and allow them to use or equip these items.

```javascript
// Example item catalog
const itemCatalog = {
  1: { name: 'Health Potion', description: 'Restores health.', price: { coins
: 20 } },
  2: { name: 'Sword of Power', description: 'Increases attack damage.', price
```

```
  : { coins: 100, gems: 5 } },
};

// Player's inventory
const playerInventory = {
  1: 5, // 5 Health Potions
};
```

3. In-Game Store:

Implement an in-game store where players can browse and purchase items using virtual currency. Ensure that the store interface is user-friendly and visually appealing.

```
// Example in-game store interface
function openStore() {
  console.log('Welcome to the in-game store!');
  console.log('Available items:');
  for (const itemId in itemCatalog) {
    const item = itemCatalog[itemId];
    console.log(`${itemId}. ${item.name} - ${item.price.coins} coins, ${item.
price.gems || 0} gems`);
  }
}

// Function to handle item purchase
function purchaseItem(itemId) {
  const item = itemCatalog[itemId];
  if (!item) {
    console.log('Item not found.');
    return;
  }

  const totalPrice = { coins: item.price.coins || 0, gems: item.price.gems ||
0 };
  if (canAfford(totalPrice)) {
    // Deduct the item price from the player's currency balance
    deductCurrency(totalPrice);
    // Add the item to the player's inventory
    playerInventory[itemId] = (playerInventory[itemId] || 0) + 1;
    console.log(`You purchased ${item.name}.`);
  } else {
    console.log('You cannot afford this item.');
  }
}
```

4. Monetization Strategies:

Consider different monetization strategies, such as selling virtual currency bundles, limited-time offers, or subscription services. Ensure that your monetization model aligns with your game's genre and target audience.

165

5. Balancing and Fairness:

Balance the economy system to ensure fair progression for both free and paying players. Avoid creating a "pay-to-win" environment that discourages non-paying players.

6. Data Security:

When implementing real-money transactions, prioritize data security and compliance with payment regulations to protect players' sensitive information.

7. User Feedback and Analytics:

Gather player feedback and analyze in-game analytics to make informed decisions about pricing, item availability, and overall economy system adjustments.

Implementing a well-designed economy system and in-game transactions can enhance player engagement and provide a source of revenue for your JavaScript game. Ensure transparency and fairness in your monetization strategies to create a positive gaming experience for all players.

Section 13.5: Adaptive Difficulty and Learning AI

Adaptive difficulty and learning AI are essential elements in modern game design. They enhance the player's experience by tailoring the game's challenge level to their skill and providing a more engaging and enjoyable gameplay experience. In this section, we'll explore how to implement adaptive difficulty and learning AI in your JavaScript game.

1. Understanding Adaptive Difficulty:

Adaptive difficulty is a game design concept that adjusts the game's challenge based on the player's performance and skill level. It aims to keep players engaged by providing an appropriate level of challenge, preventing frustration without making the game too easy. Key elements of adaptive difficulty include:

- **Player Skill Assessment:** Assess the player's skill level through in-game actions, such as their performance in battles, completion times, or achievements.

- **Dynamic Adjustments:** Modify game parameters such as enemy health, damage, or spawn rates based on the player's skill. Increase the challenge for skilled players and ease it for newcomers.

- **Feedback and Rewards:** Provide feedback to players about the difficulty adjustments and reward them for overcoming challenges.

```
// Example adaptive difficulty system
const playerSkill = calculatePlayerSkill(); // Calculate player's skill level
```

```
function adjustDifficulty() {
  if (playerSkill > 0.7) {
    // Skilled player, increase enemy health and damage
    increaseEnemyDifficulty();
  } else if (playerSkill < 0.3) {
    // Novice player, decrease enemy difficulty
    decreaseEnemyDifficulty();
  }
  // Apply other adjustments as needed
}
```

2. Learning AI:

Learning AI refers to artificial intelligence systems that adapt and improve their behavior based on the player's actions and strategies. It enhances the game's realism and challenge by creating intelligent opponents that learn from their mistakes and adapt to the player's tactics. Key aspects of learning AI include:

- **Behavior Modeling:** Implement AI behaviors that simulate learning and decision-making processes.

- **Data Collection:** Gather data on player behavior and choices during gameplay.

- **Model Training:** Use machine learning techniques to update AI models based on collected data.

- **Adaptive Responses:** Make the AI adapt its strategies over time to challenge the player effectively.

```
// Example learning AI behavior
class LearningEnemy {
  constructor() {
    this.strategies = []; // Store AI strategies
    this.currentStrategy = null; // Currently selected strategy
  }

  chooseStrategy(playerActions) {
    // Analyze player actions and choose the most effective strategy
    this.currentStrategy = this.findBestStrategy(playerActions);
  }

  updateStrategyFeedback(playerFeedback) {
    // Update the AI's strategy based on player feedback
    this.currentStrategy.adjust(playerFeedback);
  }
}
```

3. Feedback and Engagement:

Provide players with feedback on how the game adapts to their performance and how the AI learns from their actions. Clear communication about these systems can enhance player engagement and immersion.

4. Balancing Challenges:

Ensure that adaptive difficulty and learning AI strike a balance between challenging players and providing a satisfying experience. Avoid making the game too predictable or overly challenging.

5. Testing and Iteration:

Regularly test the adaptive systems and learning AI with real players to gather feedback and make iterative improvements. Adjust parameters and algorithms as needed to achieve the desired player experience.

6. Personalization:

Consider personalization features that allow players to customize the adaptive systems to their preferences, providing a more tailored experience.

7. Data Privacy and Ethics:

When collecting player data for adaptive systems, prioritize data privacy and adhere to ethical guidelines to protect player information.

Implementing adaptive difficulty and learning AI can significantly enhance your JavaScript game's replayability and player satisfaction. These systems create dynamic and engaging experiences that adapt to each player's unique skill level and style of play.

Chapter 14: Social Features and Community Building

Section 14.1: Incorporating Social Media Integration

Social media integration is a powerful tool for enhancing your game's reach and engagement. By seamlessly connecting your game to popular social media platforms, you can leverage social features to build a strong community of players and promote your game effectively. In this section, we'll explore how to incorporate social media integration into your JavaScript game.

1. Benefits of Social Media Integration:

Integrating social media into your game offers several advantages:

- **Increased Visibility:** Sharing achievements, high scores, and in-game events on social media can attract new players and create viral marketing opportunities.

- **Community Building:** Foster a sense of community among players by allowing them to connect with friends, share experiences, and compete against each other.

- **User Engagement:** Encourage players to spend more time in your game by offering social features like leaderboards, challenges, and multiplayer modes.

- **User Acquisition:** Leverage social media login and sharing features to streamline user acquisition and onboarding.

2. Popular Social Media APIs:

To integrate social media into your JavaScript game, you can use APIs provided by major platforms like Facebook, Twitter, and Instagram. These APIs offer functionalities such as sharing content, inviting friends, and accessing user profiles.

```javascript
// Example of sharing a high score on Facebook
function shareOnFacebook(score) {
  FB.api(
    '/me/feed',
    'post',
    {
      message: `I just scored ${score} points in the Awesome Game! `,
      link: 'https://yourgame.com',
    },
    (response) => {
      if (response && !response.error) {
        // Shared successfully
        console.log('Shared on Facebook');
      } else {
        // Handle error
        console.error('Failed to share on Facebook');
      }
```

```
        }
    );
}
```

3. Social Features to Implement:

Consider implementing the following social features in your game:

- **Social Sharing:** Allow players to share their achievements, high scores, or in-game items on their social media profiles.

- **Friend Invitations:** Enable players to invite their friends to join the game, offering incentives for successful referrals.

- **Leaderboards:** Display leaderboards showcasing top players and their achievements, encouraging healthy competition.

- **Social Login:** Simplify the registration and login process by allowing users to sign in with their social media accounts.

- **In-Game Chat:** Implement real-time chat functionality to facilitate communication among players.

4. Privacy and Permissions:

When integrating social media, respect user privacy and request only the necessary permissions. Be transparent about how you handle user data and adhere to platform-specific guidelines and policies.

5. Cross-Platform Integration:

Consider integrating multiple social media platforms to reach a broader audience. Ensure that your game's social features work seamlessly across various devices and browsers.

6. Analytics and Tracking:

Use analytics tools to monitor the effectiveness of your social media integration. Track user engagement, referral sources, and conversion rates to optimize your social strategies.

Incorporating social media integration can turn your JavaScript game into a social experience, fostering a loyal player community and increasing your game's visibility and reach. By leveraging the power of social media, you can create a game that players love to share and play with friends.

Section 14.2: Building Online Communities and Forums

Building an online community and forums around your JavaScript game can be a valuable asset for player engagement and retention. Communities provide a space for players to connect, share experiences, and discuss game-related topics. In this section, we'll explore how to create and maintain online communities and forums for your game.

1. Selecting a Platform:

Choose a platform or software for hosting your game's community and forums. Popular options include:

- **Discord:** Discord provides text and voice chat channels, making it a versatile choice for community building. Create a server dedicated to your game and set up channels for different topics.

- **Reddit:** Subreddits related to gaming are excellent places to host discussions about your game. Participate in existing subreddits or create a dedicated subreddit for your game.

- **Online Forums:** Consider using forum software like phpBB, vBulletin, or Discourse to create a standalone forum for your game on your website.

2. Community Guidelines:

Establish clear community guidelines and rules to maintain a positive and welcoming environment. Encourage respectful behavior, and define consequences for violations.

3. Engagement and Moderation:

Actively engage with your community members. Respond to questions, feedback, and concerns. Appoint moderators to help maintain a friendly atmosphere and enforce the rules.

4. Content Creation:

Encourage community members to create and share content related to your game. This could include fan art, guides, tutorials, and gameplay videos. Highlight exceptional user-generated content.

5. Announcements and Updates:

Use your community platform to announce game updates, patches, and upcoming events. Keep players informed about the latest developments and improvements.

6. Events and Contests:

Organize community events, contests, and challenges to keep players engaged and motivated. Offer in-game rewards or recognition to winners.

7. Q&A and Feedback Sessions:

Host Q&A sessions or ask for feedback from the community. Show that you value their input and are committed to improving the game based on their suggestions.

8. Accessibility and Inclusivity:

Ensure that your community and forums are accessible to a diverse audience. Foster inclusivity and create a welcoming environment for players of all backgrounds.

9. Integration with Game:

Consider integrating some forum or community features directly into your game. For example, you can add a link to the community forum in your game's menu or allow players to access user-generated content from within the game.

10. Analytics and Feedback Analysis:

Monitor community activity and analyze feedback to gain insights into player preferences, pain points, and suggestions. Use this information to shape future game updates.

11. Promotion and Growth:

Promote your community through in-game messages, social media, and your game's website. Encourage players to invite friends and fellow gamers to join the community.

12. Resolving Issues:

Be prepared to address conflicts and issues within the community promptly and professionally. Maintain a balance between fostering a positive environment and addressing criticism or concerns.

13. Regular Updates:

Consistently update and maintain your community platform. Ensure that it remains a vibrant and active space for players to connect and interact.

By creating a thriving online community and forums for your JavaScript game, you can strengthen player engagement, foster a sense of belonging, and facilitate discussions about your game. A well-moderated and active community can become a powerful asset for player retention and long-term success.

Section 14.3: Creating In-Game Chat Systems

Implementing an in-game chat system in your JavaScript game can enhance player interaction and provide a social dimension to the gaming experience. In this section, we will explore how to create an in-game chat system that allows players to communicate with each other seamlessly.

1. Choosing a Chat Library:

Start by selecting a JavaScript chat library or framework that suits your game's needs. Popular options include:

- **Socket.io:** Socket.io is a real-time, bidirectional communication library that is often used for chat systems in multiplayer games.

- **Firebase Realtime Database:** Firebase offers a real-time NoSQL database that can be used to build chat features. It's easy to integrate with JavaScript.

- **Custom Implementation:** If you prefer more control, you can implement a custom chat system using WebSockets for real-time communication.

2. User Authentication:

Ensure that users are authenticated before they can access the chat system. Use a secure authentication method, such as OAuth, to validate users' identities.

3. Creating Chat Rooms:

Organize chat conversations into rooms or channels. For example, you can have global chat rooms, private messaging, and chat rooms dedicated to specific in-game events.

4. Message Formatting:

Implement a message formatting system to allow users to send messages with various styles, such as bold, italic, or code blocks. You can use Markdown or a similar syntax for formatting.

5. Real-Time Updates:

Utilize the chosen library to enable real-time updates for chat messages. When a player sends a message, it should appear immediately for others in the same chat room.

6. Moderation and Filtering:

Implement moderation features to prevent abuse and inappropriate content. You can use profanity filters and allow players to report abusive behavior.

7. Message History:

Store chat message history to allow players to view previous messages when they join a chat room. This helps new players catch up on ongoing conversations.

8. Notifications:

Implement notifications to alert users when they receive new messages, especially if they are currently playing the game in full-screen mode.

9. Emojis and Reactions:

Enhance chat interactions by allowing users to send emojis and reactions to messages. This adds a layer of expressiveness to conversations.

10. Integration with User Interface:

Integrate the chat system with your game's user interface (UI). Add a chat window or panel where players can type and view messages without leaving the game.

11. Private Messaging:

Implement private messaging features that allow players to send direct messages to each other. Ensure that private conversations remain secure and cannot be accessed by unauthorized users.

12. Cross-Platform Compatibility:

If your game is available on multiple platforms (e.g., web, mobile), ensure that the in-game chat system works seamlessly across all platforms.

13. Scalability:

Design the chat system to be scalable to handle a growing player base. Ensure that it can handle a large number of concurrent users without performance issues.

14. Testing and Feedback:

Thoroughly test the chat system in various scenarios, and gather feedback from players to identify any issues or areas for improvement.

15. Data Privacy and Security:

Pay attention to data privacy and security. Encrypt messages and sensitive user data to protect player privacy.

16. Maintenance and Updates:

Regularly maintain and update the chat system to address bugs, security vulnerabilities, and to introduce new features based on player feedback.

By implementing an in-game chat system, you can create a sense of community among your players, encourage collaboration, and make your game more engaging and social. An effective chat system can contribute significantly to the overall player experience and satisfaction.

Section 14.4: Organizing Online Events and Tournaments

Organizing online events and tournaments can be a great way to engage your gaming community and keep players excited about your game. In this section, we will discuss how to plan and execute successful online events and tournaments for your JavaScript game.

1. Setting Objectives:

Before you start planning an event or tournament, define your objectives. Are you aiming to increase player engagement, promote your game, or celebrate a milestone? Clear objectives will guide your event planning.

2. Choosing Event Types:

Decide what type of event or tournament you want to host. Some common types include:

- **Single-player challenges:** Time-based speed runs, high score competitions, or solo quests.
- **Multiplayer tournaments:** PvP (player vs. player) or co-op tournaments.
- **Community events:** Events that encourage collaboration and social interaction among players.

3. Scheduling:

Select the date and time for your event. Consider time zones to accommodate a global player base. Make sure the schedule aligns with your target audience's availability.

4. Promotion:

Promote your event well in advance. Utilize your game's website, social media channels, and mailing lists to spread the word. Create eye-catching graphics and teasers to generate excitement.

5. Registration:

If your event requires registration, provide a simple and user-friendly registration process. Gather necessary information and communicate event details to registered participants.

6. Prizes and Rewards:

Determine what prizes or rewards participants can earn. Prizes can include in-game items, digital badges, or physical merchandise. Ensure that the rewards are enticing to motivate players.

7. Event Rules and Guidelines:

Clearly outline the rules and guidelines of the event or tournament. Include details on scoring, gameplay mechanics, and any restrictions. Make these rules easily accessible to participants.

8. Event Hosting Platform:

Choose a reliable platform to host your event. Consider using third-party platforms specifically designed for organizing online tournaments. These platforms often provide tools for bracket generation and tracking scores.

9. Communication Channels:

Set up dedicated communication channels for participants. Create a forum, chat room, or Discord server where players can ask questions, discuss strategies, and share their experiences.

10. Live Streams and Commentary:

If possible, consider live streaming the event or providing commentary. This adds an extra layer of excitement and allows spectators to follow the action in real-time.

11. Support and Moderation:

Assign moderators or administrators to oversee the event and ensure fair play. They can also assist with technical issues and address player concerns promptly.

12. Scoring and Leaderboards:

Implement a scoring system and leaderboards that participants can check to track their progress. Real-time leaderboards can intensify competition.

13. Post-Event Analysis:

After the event concludes, analyze its success. Review player feedback, participation rates, and any technical issues. Use this feedback to improve future events.

14. Community Feedback:

Engage with your community to gather feedback about the event. Ask for suggestions on how to make future events even more exciting and engaging.

15. Documentation:

Document the event's results and share them with participants. Celebrate the winners and highlight memorable moments. This documentation can serve as a promotional tool for future events.

16. Iterate and Improve:

Based on the feedback and insights gained from each event, iterate and improve your future events. This continuous improvement process can lead to more successful and engaging tournaments.

Online events and tournaments can foster a sense of competitiveness, camaraderie, and excitement within your gaming community. They provide an opportunity to showcase your game, reward dedicated players, and create memorable experiences that keep players coming back for more.

Section 14.5: Encouraging User-Generated Content

User-generated content (UGC) is a powerful way to enrich your game's community, extend its lifespan, and increase player engagement. In this section, we'll explore strategies for encouraging and managing UGC in your JavaScript game.

1. User-Friendly Level Editors:

If your game allows players to create levels or content, ensure that your level editor is user-friendly. Provide intuitive tools and tutorials to help players get started with content creation. Consider incorporating drag-and-drop interfaces and visual scripting to simplify the process.

2. Workshops and Sharing Platforms:

Create platforms or workshops where players can showcase their UGC. Implement features that allow players to upload and share their creations easily. Consider integrating with popular gaming platforms or social media for broader exposure.

3. Community Challenges:

Host regular UGC challenges or contests that encourage players to create and submit content within specific themes or constraints. Offer rewards or recognition to top contributors to incentivize participation.

4. Collaborative Projects:

Foster collaboration among players by facilitating joint UGC projects. These projects can include creating custom maps, mods, or even entirely new game modes. Encourage players to team up and share responsibilities.

5. UGC Spotlight:

Highlight outstanding user-generated content within your game or on your website. Showcase the best player-created levels, skins, or modifications to inspire others and recognize talented creators.

6. Community Feedback:

Regularly seek feedback from your community regarding their UGC experiences. Use surveys, forums, or in-game feedback forms to gather input. This feedback can help you tailor your UGC features to better meet player expectations.

7. UGC Tutorials and Resources:

Provide tutorials and resources for creating UGC. Publish guides, video tutorials, or documentation that explain the UGC creation process step by step. Empowering your players with knowledge will encourage more UGC contributions.

8. UGC Integration:

Consider integrating UGC directly into your game's ecosystem. Allow players to access and play community-created content seamlessly from within the game. Implement features like rating, commenting, and favoriting to enhance the UGC experience.

9. UGC Moderation:

Establish moderation systems to ensure that inappropriate or harmful content doesn't make its way into the UGC ecosystem. This includes both automated filters and human moderators who can review and remove content violating your guidelines.

10. UGC Events and Showcases:

Organize events or showcases specifically dedicated to UGC. Host live streams, developer commentary sessions, or community events that revolve around player-created content. Make these events memorable and inclusive.

11. UGC Monetization:

Explore opportunities for UGC monetization, such as allowing creators to sell their content through in-game marketplaces. Implement revenue-sharing models that reward content creators for their contributions.

12. UGC Analytics:

Leverage analytics to understand how players engage with UGC. Track metrics such as content creation rates, download counts, and user engagement to gain insights into what works and what can be improved.

13. UGC Challenges and Achievements:

Incorporate UGC-related challenges and achievements within your game. Reward players for creating, sharing, or engaging with user-generated content. This gamification can encourage more UGC involvement.

14. Developer Involvement:

Showcase developer support for UGC by creating your own content and participating in UGC challenges. This can inspire players and demonstrate your commitment to the UGC community.

15. UGC Updates and Expansions:

Regularly update your game to include new features, tools, and assets that empower UGC creators. Keep your UGC community engaged by expanding their creative possibilities.

16. UGC Feedback Loop:

Maintain an ongoing feedback loop with UGC creators. Actively listen to their suggestions, address issues, and implement requested features whenever possible. This demonstrates that you value their contributions.

Encouraging user-generated content can transform your game into a vibrant and evolving community-driven experience. By fostering creativity and engagement among your players, you can extend the longevity and appeal of your JavaScript game.

Chapter 15: Game Optimization and Scalability

Section 15.1: Code Refactoring for Better Performance

Optimizing your JavaScript game's performance is crucial to ensure it runs smoothly on various devices and platforms. One of the key strategies for achieving better performance is code refactoring. In this section, we'll explore the importance of code refactoring and provide tips on how to refactor your game code effectively.

1. Identify Performance Bottlenecks:

Before you start refactoring, it's essential to identify performance bottlenecks in your game. Use profiling tools like the Chrome DevTools' Performance tab or third-party tools like Lighthouse to pinpoint areas of your code that need improvement. Common bottlenecks include excessive DOM manipulation, inefficient algorithms, and memory leaks.

2. Set Clear Performance Goals:

Define clear performance goals for your game. Determine the target frame rate and load times you want to achieve. Having specific goals will guide your refactoring efforts and help you measure success.

3. Prioritize Refactoring Tasks:

Not all parts of your codebase may require immediate attention. Prioritize refactoring tasks based on their impact on performance and user experience. Focus on critical areas first, and gradually work your way through less critical components.

4. Modularize Your Code:

Break your code into smaller, reusable modules. Modularization not only improves code organization but also makes it easier to identify and isolate performance issues within specific modules. Use tools like Webpack or ES6 modules for efficient code structuring.

5. Optimize Loops and Iterations:

Loops and iterations are common sources of performance problems. Look for opportunities to optimize loops by reducing unnecessary iterations and avoiding repeated calculations. Use techniques like memoization and caching to improve loop efficiency.

6. Minimize DOM Manipulation:

Excessive DOM manipulation can lead to performance bottlenecks, especially in browser-based games. Minimize DOM updates by batching changes, using document fragments, or leveraging virtual DOM libraries like React or Vue.js.

7. Implement Lazy Loading:

Load assets, such as images and audio, lazily as needed rather than upfront. This reduces initial loading times and memory usage. Consider implementing asynchronous loading techniques and optimizing asset formats for smaller file sizes.

8. Use Efficient Data Structures:

Choose the right data structures for your game logic. Arrays, maps, and sets can have different performance characteristics for specific tasks. Opt for data structures that provide the fastest access times and minimize memory overhead.

9. Reduce Memory Leaks:

Memory leaks can degrade performance over time. Regularly audit your code for memory leaks, especially in long-running games. Use memory profiling tools to identify and fix leaks caused by forgotten references or event listeners.

10. Eliminate Redundant Code:

Review your codebase for redundant or duplicated code. Repeated code segments can lead to maintenance challenges and performance issues. Refactor redundant code into reusable functions or classes.

11. Optimize Asset Loading:

Optimize the loading and handling of game assets. Use image sprites, texture atlases, and audio sprite sheets to reduce the number of server requests. Compress and cache assets to minimize load times.

12. Profile and Test Continuously:

Regularly profile your game's performance using tools like Chrome DevTools. Test your game on various devices and browsers to ensure consistent performance. Consider setting up automated performance tests as part of your development pipeline.

13. Monitor and Analyze Metrics:

Implement performance monitoring and analytics to track your game's performance in real-world scenarios. Collect data on frame rates, load times, and memory usage. Use this data to make informed decisions about further optimizations.

14. Document Your Refactoring:

As you refactor your code, document the changes you make and the reasons behind them. This documentation will help your team understand the optimizations and facilitate future maintenance.

15. Seek Community Feedback:

Engage with your game's community to gather feedback on performance improvements. Players may notice performance issues that you haven't identified. Actively address reported issues to enhance the user experience.

Code refactoring for performance is an ongoing process. Continuously monitor and improve your game's performance to ensure it provides a smooth and enjoyable experience for players across different devices and platforms.

Section 15.2: Memory Management and Leak Prevention

Efficient memory management is critical for the performance and stability of your JavaScript game. Memory leaks can lead to gradual performance degradation and, in some cases, crashes. In this section, we'll explore memory management best practices and techniques to prevent memory leaks in your game code.

1. Understand JavaScript's Garbage Collection:

JavaScript employs automatic garbage collection to reclaim memory from objects that are no longer in use. Familiarize yourself with how garbage collection works in your chosen JavaScript environment, as it can vary between browsers and platforms.

2. Minimize Global Variables:

Excessive global variables can prevent objects from being garbage collected, leading to memory leaks. Limit the use of global variables and use local variables or properties within objects when possible.

```
// Global variable
let globalVar = {};

// Better: Local variable
function myFunction() {
  let localVar = {};
}
```

3. Clean Up Event Listeners:

Event listeners can be a common source of memory leaks if not removed properly. When adding event listeners to DOM elements, ensure you remove them when they are no longer needed, such as when an element is removed from the DOM.

```
// Potential memory leak
element.addEventListener('click', myHandler);
```

```
// Remove event listener when no longer needed
element.removeEventListener('click', myHandler);
```

4. Avoid Circular References:

Circular references, where objects reference each other, can prevent garbage collection. Be cautious when designing your game architecture to avoid unintentional circular references. When you're done with an object, nullify any references to it.

```
// Circular reference
function createCircularReference() {
  const obj1 = {};
  const obj2 = {};
  obj1.reference = obj2;
  obj2.reference = obj1;
}
```

5. Use WeakMap and WeakSet:

JavaScript provides WeakMap and WeakSet data structures that can be used to store weak references to objects. Weak references won't prevent objects from being garbage collected when there are no strong references left.

```
const weakMap = new WeakMap();

const obj = {};
weakMap.set(obj, 'Some value');
```

6. Monitor Memory Usage:

Leverage browser developer tools to monitor memory usage in your game. The Chrome DevTools' Memory tab, for example, can help identify memory leaks by tracking memory snapshots and allocations.

7. Implement Object Pooling:

In scenarios where you frequently create and destroy objects, consider implementing an object pooling system. Object pooling reuses existing objects instead of creating new ones, reducing memory allocation and deallocation overhead.

```
// Object pooling example
const objectPool = [];

function createObject() {
  if (objectPool.length > 0) {
    return objectPool.pop();
  } else {
    return {};
  }
}
```

```
function releaseObject(obj) {
  // Reset object properties and return it to the pool
  // ...
  objectPool.push(obj);
}
```

8. Regularly Test for Leaks:

Perform memory leak testing as part of your development and testing processes. Tools like the JavaScript library `memory-leak-detector` can automate memory leak detection in your game.

9. Avoid Heavy DOM Manipulation:

Excessive DOM manipulation, especially when creating and removing elements frequently, can lead to memory leaks. Minimize direct DOM manipulation and use libraries like React or Vue.js to handle DOM updates efficiently.

10. Profile Memory Usage:

Profile your game's memory usage using tools like Chrome DevTools or browser extensions like "The Great Suspender." Identify areas of your code that consume significant memory and optimize them.

Efficient memory management and leak prevention are crucial for maintaining your game's performance and stability over time. Regularly review and refactor your code to address any memory-related issues and ensure a smooth gaming experience for your players.

Section 15.3: Scalable Game Architectures

Scalability is a fundamental consideration when developing JavaScript games, especially for web-based games that may need to accommodate varying numbers of players and different levels of complexity. A scalable game architecture allows your game to handle increased loads and adapt to changing requirements without sacrificing performance or user experience.

1. Client-Server Architecture:

One common approach to scalability is using a client-server architecture. In this model, the game logic runs on a server, while clients (players) connect to the server to interact with the game. This separation allows for easy scaling of server resources as player numbers increase.

2. Load Balancing:

Implement load balancing to distribute incoming connections and game sessions across multiple server instances. Load balancers help prevent any single server from becoming a bottleneck and ensure even resource utilization.

```
// Example using Node.js and the 'http' module
const http = require('http');
const cluster = require('cluster');
const numCPUs = require('os').cpus().length;

if (cluster.isMaster) {
  // Fork workers for each CPU core
  for (let i = 0; i < numCPUs; i++) {
    cluster.fork();
  }

  cluster.on('exit', (worker, code, signal) => {
    console.log(`Worker ${worker.process.pid} died`);
  });
} else {
  // Create an HTTP server for each worker
  const server = http.createServer((req, res) => {
    // Handle incoming requests
    // ...
  });

  server.listen(8000, () => {
    console.log(`Server running on port 8000`);
  });
}
```

3. Database Scaling:

Games often require database storage for player data, leaderboards, and more. Choose a database system that supports horizontal scaling, such as NoSQL databases or distributed databases like Cassandra.

4. Caching:

Utilize caching mechanisms to store frequently accessed data in memory, reducing the load on the database and improving response times. Technologies like Redis or Memcached are popular choices for caching.

5. Microservices:

Consider breaking down your game's functionality into microservices, which are independently deployable and scalable components. Each microservice can handle specific tasks, such as player authentication, chat, or in-game purchases.

185

6. WebSockets and Real-Time Communication:

For real-time multiplayer games, implement WebSockets to establish low-latency communication between clients and the server. WebSockets are well-suited for maintaining synchronized game states.

```
// Example using the 'ws' library in Node.js
const WebSocket = require('ws');
const wss = new WebSocket.Server({ port: 8080 });

wss.on('connection', (ws) => {
  // Handle WebSocket connections
  ws.on('message', (message) => {
    // Process incoming messages
    // ...
  });
});
```

7. Content Delivery Networks (CDNs):

Leverage CDNs to distribute game assets, such as images, audio, and scripts, to players from servers geographically closer to them. CDNs improve loading times and reduce the load on your game server.

8. Serverless Computing:

Consider serverless computing platforms like AWS Lambda or Azure Functions for handling specific game-related tasks, such as processing player uploads or sending email notifications. Serverless functions automatically scale with demand.

9. Monitoring and Autoscaling:

Implement monitoring and autoscaling solutions to automatically adjust the number of server instances based on traffic and resource utilization. Cloud providers offer tools like AWS Auto Scaling and Google Cloud's Compute Engine Autoscaler.

10. Testing Scalability:

Regularly test your game's scalability using load testing tools to simulate heavy player loads and identify potential bottlenecks. Testing helps ensure your game can handle peak usage scenarios.

Scalability is an ongoing concern, and it's crucial to continually assess and adapt your game architecture as your player base grows and technology evolves. By implementing scalable architectures and best practices, you can provide a smooth and enjoyable gaming experience for all your players, whether your game has a handful of users or millions.

Section 15.4: Load Balancing and Resource Management

Load balancing and resource management are essential components of a scalable game architecture, ensuring that your game can handle increasing player loads without degrading performance or causing server failures. In this section, we'll explore load balancing strategies and resource management techniques to optimize your game's scalability.

1. Load Balancing Strategies:

Load balancing is the process of distributing incoming network traffic and game sessions across multiple servers. The goal is to prevent any single server from becoming overwhelmed and to evenly distribute the load. There are several load balancing strategies to consider:

- **Round Robin:** The simplest method, where incoming requests are distributed in a cyclical manner to available servers.

- **Least Connections:** New connections are directed to the server with the fewest active connections, ensuring an even distribution of work.

- **Weighted Round Robin:** Assigns weights to servers to control the distribution of traffic. Servers with higher weights receive more connections.

- **Session Persistence:** Also known as sticky sessions, this strategy routes requests from the same client to the same server to maintain session data continuity.

2. Load Balancing Technologies:

Various load balancing technologies and solutions are available, depending on your game's architecture:

- **Hardware Load Balancers:** Physical devices optimized for load balancing and often used in data centers.

- **Software Load Balancers:** Software-based solutions that can be deployed on virtual machines or containers.

- **Content Delivery Networks (CDNs):** CDNs provide load balancing for distributing game assets, such as images, audio, and scripts, closer to players.

3. Auto Scaling:

Auto scaling is a critical feature in cloud environments. It allows your infrastructure to automatically adjust the number of server instances based on traffic and resource utilization. Popular cloud providers like AWS, Google Cloud, and Azure offer auto scaling services that enable your game servers to scale up or down as needed.

```
// Example auto scaling policy using AWS Auto Scaling
{
```

```
"ResourceType": "AWS::EC2::AutoScalingGroup",
"ScalingAdjustment": 1, // Increase the instance count by 1
"AdjustmentType": "ChangeInCapacity",
"Cooldown": 300 // Cooldown period in seconds
}
```

4. Resource Monitoring:

Effective load balancing and resource management require continuous monitoring of server performance and player traffic. Tools like Amazon CloudWatch, Google Cloud Monitoring, or third-party monitoring services can provide real-time insights into your game's resource utilization, enabling proactive adjustments.

5. Resource Pooling:

Resource pooling involves aggregating and sharing computing resources across multiple servers. This approach allows servers to dynamically allocate resources based on demand. For example, a server might allocate more CPU and memory resources to a specific game instance during peak gameplay.

6. Database Scaling:

Scaling your game's database is crucial for managing player data and leaderboards. Consider using databases that support horizontal scaling, such as NoSQL databases or distributed databases like Cassandra.

7. Content Delivery Networks (CDNs):

CDNs not only distribute game assets but also help with load balancing by directing player requests to the nearest server location. CDNs optimize content delivery and reduce the load on your game servers.

8. Error Handling and Failover:

Implement error handling and failover mechanisms to gracefully handle server failures. When a server becomes unavailable, traffic should be redirected to healthy servers to minimize downtime.

Load balancing and resource management are integral to ensuring that your game remains responsive and available, even during traffic spikes. By carefully planning your load balancing strategy, monitoring resource utilization, and using auto scaling features, you can create a scalable game infrastructure that adapts to player demand while maintaining a high-quality gaming experience.

Section 15.5: Preparing for High Traffic and User Loads

Preparing your game for high traffic and user loads is a crucial aspect of game development. As your game gains popularity, you'll need to ensure that your infrastructure can handle a large number of concurrent players without performance issues or downtime. In this section, we'll explore strategies and techniques for scaling your game to meet the demands of a growing player base.

1. Load Testing:

Load testing involves simulating a large number of concurrent players to assess how your game and infrastructure perform under heavy loads. Tools like Apache JMeter, LoadRunner, or custom scripts can be used to create realistic load scenarios. By identifying bottlenecks and performance issues early, you can optimize your game's architecture.

```
// Example load testing script using Apache JMeter
Thread Group: Number of Threads (Users) = 1000
HTTP Request: Simulate player actions (e.g., login, gameplay)
```

2. Caching:

Implement caching mechanisms to reduce the load on your backend servers. Caching frequently accessed data, such as player profiles, leaderboards, or static game assets, can significantly improve response times and reduce database queries.

```
// Example caching using Redis
const redis = require('redis');
const client = redis.createClient();

// Cache player profile data for 10 minutes
client.setex('player_profile:12345', 600, JSON.stringify(playerData));

// Retrieve player profile from cache
client.get('player_profile:12345', (err, data) => {
  if (!err && data) {
    const profile = JSON.parse(data);
    // Use cached data
  } else {
    // Fetch data from the database and update the cache
  }
});
```

3. Content Delivery Networks (CDNs):

Leverage CDNs to distribute game assets, reducing the load on your game servers. CDNs provide low-latency access to assets for players worldwide by caching and delivering content from edge locations.

4. Database Optimization:

Optimize database queries and indexing to handle increased player data and leaderboard updates. Implement database sharding or partitioning strategies to distribute data across multiple database instances.

```sql
-- Example SQL query optimization
SELECT * FROM player_scores WHERE game_id = 12345 ORDER BY score DESC LIMIT 1
0;
-- Ensure an index on (game_id, score) for efficient leaderboard queries
```

5. Scalable Server Architecture:

Use cloud-based solutions like AWS, Google Cloud, or Azure to build a scalable server architecture. Auto-scaling and load balancing features allow your game to adapt to changing player loads automatically.

```
// Example auto scaling policy using AWS Auto Scaling
{
  "ResourceType": "AWS::EC2::AutoScalingGroup",
  "ScalingAdjustment": 1, // Increase the instance count by 1
  "AdjustmentType": "ChangeInCapacity",
  "Cooldown": 300 // Cooldown period in seconds
}
```

6. Monitoring and Alerts:

Set up monitoring and alerting systems to detect and respond to performance anomalies in real-time. Services like Amazon CloudWatch or Google Cloud Monitoring can help you track server metrics and receive notifications.

7. Disaster Recovery Plan:

Create a disaster recovery plan to mitigate the impact of unexpected outages. Regularly back up game data and configurations, and have procedures in place for quickly restoring services.

8. Scaling Horizontally:

Consider horizontal scaling by adding more game servers to distribute player connections. Use containerization technologies like Docker and Kubernetes to manage server instances efficiently.

9. Network Optimization:

Optimize your game's network traffic to minimize latency. Use content compression and efficient protocols for communication between clients and servers.

Preparing for high traffic and user loads is an ongoing process that requires continuous monitoring and optimization. By load testing, implementing caching, optimizing databases, and using scalable server architectures, you can ensure that your game can handle large player populations while delivering a smooth and enjoyable gaming experience.

Chapter 16: Monetization Strategies

Section 16.1: Understanding Different Monetization Models

Monetization is a critical aspect of game development, as it enables developers to earn revenue from their hard work and creativity. There are various monetization models available for game developers, each with its own advantages and considerations. In this section, we will explore the different monetization models commonly used in the gaming industry.

1. Freemium Model

The freemium model is one of the most popular monetization strategies for mobile games. In this model, the base game is free to download and play, but developers offer in-app purchases (IAPs) for various virtual goods, currency, or premium features within the game. Players have the option to make purchases to enhance their gaming experience or progress faster. Freemium games often use timers or energy systems to encourage players to make purchases to continue playing.

```javascript
// Example of in-app purchase prompt
function showInAppPurchasePrompt(itemName, price) {
  // Display a prompt to the player with the item name and price
  console.log(`Would you like to buy ${itemName} for $${price}?`);
  // Handle the purchase logic here
}
```

2. Advertising Model

The advertising model involves displaying ads within the game to generate revenue. There are different types of ads, including interstitial ads, rewarded video ads, and banner ads. Developers can partner with ad networks like Google AdMob or Unity Ads to integrate ads into their games. Players can choose to watch ads voluntarily in exchange for in-game rewards or currency.

```javascript
// Example of showing a rewarded video ad
function showRewardedVideoAd() {
  // Request and display a rewarded video ad
  adNetwork.showRewardedVideoAd({
    onSuccess: function () {
      // Reward the player for watching the ad
      player.addCoins(50);
    },
    onError: function () {
      // Handle ad error
    },
  });
}
```

3. Premium Model

The premium model involves selling the game upfront for a fixed price. Players pay for the game once and gain access to the full gaming experience without any additional in-game purchases or ads. Premium games often target a niche audience willing to pay for high-quality content. Pricing strategies may include one-time purchases or tiered pricing for different editions of the game.

```
// Example of offering different game editions
const gameEditions = {
  standard: {
    price: 19.99,
    features: ["Full game access"],
  },
  deluxe: {
    price: 29.99,
    features: ["Full game access", "Exclusive content"],
  },
};

// Display available editions to the player
function showGameEditions() {
  console.log("Available game editions:");
  for (const edition in gameEditions) {
    console.log(`${edition}: $${gameEditions[edition].price}`);
  }
}
```

4. Subscription Model

The subscription model involves offering players ongoing access to a game or a set of premium features for a recurring fee. This model is commonly used in massively multiplayer online games (MMOs) and subscription-based gaming platforms. Subscriptions can provide a stable source of revenue and ongoing engagement with players.

```
// Example of offering a game subscription
const subscriptionPlans = {
  monthly: {
    price: 9.99,
    features: ["Unlimited game access", "Exclusive content"],
  },
  yearly: {
    price: 99.99,
    features: ["Unlimited game access", "Exclusive content", "Discounts"],
  },
};

// Display available subscription plans to the player
function showSubscriptionPlans() {
  console.log("Available subscription plans:");
```

```javascript
for (const plan in subscriptionPlans) {
    console.log(`${plan}: $${subscriptionPlans[plan].price} per month`);
  }
}
```

5. Crowdfunding Model

The crowdfunding model involves raising funds from players and fans before the game's development. Developers use platforms like Kickstarter or Indiegogo to create campaigns and offer rewards to backers. Backers contribute funds to support the game's development, and in return, they may receive exclusive in-game items, early access, or other rewards.

```javascript
// Example of a crowdfunding campaign
function startCrowdfundingCampaign(goalAmount, rewards) {
  // Create a campaign on a crowdfunding platform
  console.log(`Help us reach our goal of $${goalAmount}!`);
  console.log("Backers can receive the following rewards:");
  for (const reward of rewards) {
    console.log(`${reward.description} for $${reward.price}`);
  }
}
```

These are just a few of the monetization models available to game developers. Choosing the right model depends on your target audience, game type, and development goals. It's essential to strike a balance between generating revenue and providing an enjoyable gaming experience for your players.

Section 16.2: Implementing Ads and In-App Purchases

Monetizing a game through ads and in-app purchases (IAPs) can be an effective strategy to generate revenue. In this section, we'll explore how to implement both advertising and IAPs in your game.

Implementing Advertising

1. Choose an Ad Network

To start implementing ads, you'll need to choose an ad network such as Google AdMob, Unity Ads, or Facebook Audience Network. Each network has its own integration process and revenue-sharing model.

2. Integrate the Ad SDK

Once you've chosen an ad network, you'll need to integrate its SDK (Software Development Kit) into your game. This typically involves adding the SDK files to your project and configuring them.

To display ads in your game, you can use ad units such as interstitial ads, rewarded video ads, or banner ads. You'll need to write code to request and display these ads at appropriate moments in your game. For example, you can show a rewarded video ad when a player wants to earn extra in-game currency.

```
// Example of showing a rewarded video ad
function showRewardedVideoAd() {
  // Request and display a rewarded video ad
  adNetwork.showRewardedVideoAd({
    onSuccess: function () {
      // Reward the player for watching the ad
      player.addCoins(50);
    },
    onError: function () {
      // Handle ad error
    },
  });
}
```

4. Handle Ad Events

Ad networks provide callbacks to handle events like ad loading, ad completion, or ad errors. You should implement logic to handle these events gracefully in your game.

Implementing In-App Purchases (IAPs)

1. Set Up an IAP Store

To sell virtual goods, currency, or premium features in your game, you need to set up an in-game store. This store will list the items available for purchase, along with their prices.

2. Integrate an IAP Library

You'll need to integrate an IAP library or use a platform-specific solution to handle in-app purchases. Libraries like Unity IAP or In-App Purchase for iOS and Android provide methods for purchasing items.

3. Create IAP Items

Define the virtual items or features that players can purchase. Each item should have a unique identifier, a name, a price, and possibly a description.

```
// Example of defining an IAP item
const iapItems = {
  coins_100: {
    id: 'coins_100',
    name: '100 Coins',
    price: 1.99,
    description: 'Get 100 coins to spend in-game.',
```

```
    },
    premium_pack: {
      id: 'premium_pack',
      name: 'Premium Pack',
      price: 4.99,
      description: 'Unlock exclusive premium content.',
    },
};
```

4. Handle Purchases

Implement code to handle the purchase flow when a player decides to buy an IAP item.
You'll need to validate the purchase with the respective app store and grant the purchased
item to the player.

```
// Example of handling an IAP purchase
function purchaseItem(itemId) {
  iapLibrary.purchaseItem({
    itemId: itemId,
    onSuccess: function () {
      // Grant the purchased item to the player
      player.giveItem(itemId);
    },
    onError: function () {
      // Handle purchase error
    },
  });
}
```

5. Restore Purchases

Provide an option for players to restore their purchases if they switch devices or reinstall
the game. This ensures they can access their previously purchased items.

```
// Example of restoring purchases
function restorePurchases() {
  iapLibrary.restorePurchases({
    onSuccess: function (purchasedItems) {
      // Grant the restored items to the player
      player.restoreItems(purchasedItems);
    },
    onError: function () {
      // Handle restore error
    },
  });
}
```

Balancing Ads and IAPs

A successful monetization strategy often involves finding the right balance between ads
and in-app purchases. You should consider player experience and avoid overwhelming

users with too many ads or aggressive IAP prompts. Strive to create a fair and enjoyable gameplay experience while generating revenue for your game.

Section 16.3: Subscription Models and Premium Features

In the realm of mobile game monetization, subscription models and premium features offer distinct approaches to generating revenue. In this section, we'll delve into the implementation of subscription-based monetization and the integration of premium features in your game.

Subscription Models

1. Choose a Subscription Model

When considering subscription-based monetization, you have various models to choose from, such as:

- **Tiered Subscriptions:** Offering multiple subscription tiers with different benefits.
- **Free Trial Periods:** Allowing users to try your premium content before subscribing.
- **Auto-Renewable Subscriptions:** Subscriptions that renew automatically until canceled by the user.

2. Integrate Subscription Services

To implement subscription models, you'll need to integrate the services provided by app stores (e.g., Apple's StoreKit and Google Play Billing). These services handle the billing and subscription management.

3. Create Subscription Benefits

Define the benefits of subscribing to your game. These could include ad removal, access to premium content, faster progression, or exclusive in-game items.

4. Display Subscription Offers

Design and display subscription offers within your game's user interface. Make sure users understand the value they'll receive by subscribing.

5. Trial Periods

If you offer free trial periods, ensure they are compelling and provide users with a taste of the premium experience. Clearly communicate when the trial period ends and the subscription begins.

Premium Features

1. Identify Premium Content

Premium features are additional game elements or content that players can unlock through a one-time purchase. Determine which game elements you'll designate as premium.

2. Implement Unlocking Mechanisms

Create the mechanisms to unlock premium content upon purchase. This might involve changing the state of the game to grant access to new levels, characters, or items.

3. Premium Currency

Introduce a premium currency that can be bought with real money and used to unlock premium features. Ensure a clear conversion rate between real currency and premium currency.

4. In-Game Store

Implement an in-game store where players can browse and purchase premium content. This store should be easy to navigate and understand.

5. Promotions and Discounts

Periodically offer promotions or discounts on premium content to encourage purchases. Limited-time offers can create a sense of urgency.

Balancing Subscriptions and Premium Features

Balancing subscription models and premium features requires careful consideration. Some players prefer one-time purchases for permanent access to content, while others appreciate the ongoing value of subscriptions. Striking a balance between these approaches can maximize your game's monetization while keeping players engaged and satisfied.

Section 16.4: Crowdfunding and Early Access Campaigns

Crowdfunding and early access campaigns are alternative monetization strategies that involve the community and player base in the development process. In this section, we'll explore how you can utilize these approaches effectively.

Crowdfunding Campaigns

Crowdfunding platforms like Kickstarter and Indiegogo have become popular for game developers seeking financial support and community engagement. Here's how to run a successful crowdfunding campaign for your game:

1. Preparation

- **Set Clear Goals:** Define the purpose of your campaign and what you intend to achieve with the funds.
- **Create a Compelling Pitch:** Craft a persuasive pitch that explains your game's concept, features, and why people should support it.
- **Rewards Tiers:** Offer enticing rewards for backers at different contribution levels, including exclusive in-game items or early access.

2. Campaign Launch

- **Timing:** Choose the timing of your campaign carefully, considering factors like industry events and holidays.
- **Marketing:** Promote your campaign through social media, email lists, and gaming forums to reach potential backers.

3. Community Engagement

- **Engage with Backers:** Respond promptly to questions and comments from backers to build trust and rapport.
- **Updates:** Regularly update backers on your progress and any significant developments related to the game.

4. Fulfillment

- **Delivery:** Ensure you can fulfill rewards and deliver them as promised.
- **Transparency:** Maintain transparency throughout the development process, including any setbacks or challenges.

Early Access Campaigns

Early access allows players to purchase and play your game while it's still in development. Here's how to leverage early access effectively:

1. Early Access Strategy

- **Playable Build:** Release an early, playable build of your game that showcases core gameplay elements.
- **Roadmap:** Share a development roadmap outlining planned updates and improvements.

2. Community Involvement

- **Feedback Channels:** Create dedicated channels for players to provide feedback, report bugs, and suggest improvements.
- **Listening to Players:** Actively listen to player feedback and make meaningful changes based on their input.

3. Regular Updates

- **Consistent Updates:** Regularly release updates, fixes, and new content to keep players engaged.

- **Transparency:** Be open about the development process, acknowledging both successes and challenges.

4. Pricing

- **Pricing Strategy:** Determine a fair price for your early access game based on its current state and planned features.
- **Discounts:** Consider offering discounts to early access players as a gesture of appreciation for their support.

5. Community Building

- **Community Forums:** Set up forums or discussion platforms where players can interact with each other and the development team.
- **Events:** Organize special in-game events or challenges to foster community engagement.

Both crowdfunding and early access campaigns require effective communication and community management. By involving players in the development process, you can create a dedicated and supportive player base that not only contributes financially but also provides valuable feedback and helps spread the word about your game.

Section 16.5: Analyzing Revenue Data and Maximizing Profits

Analyzing revenue data and maximizing profits are essential aspects of game development, especially when it comes to sustaining and growing your game's success. In this section, we'll explore strategies for revenue analysis and optimization.

Revenue Analysis

1. Data Collection and Tracking

- **Implement Analytics Tools:** Integrate analytics platforms such as Google Analytics, Firebase Analytics, or custom solutions to track player behavior, purchases, and in-game events.
- **In-App Purchase Data:** Monitor data related to in-app purchases, including conversion rates, purchase frequency, and average transaction value.

2. Player Segmentation

- **Segment Players:** Categorize players into different groups based on their behavior, spending habits, and engagement levels.
- **Targeted Messaging:** Use player segments to deliver targeted in-game promotions, offers, or ads.

3. A/B Testing

- **Experimentation:** Conduct A/B tests to evaluate different monetization strategies, pricing models, and ad placements.
- **Data-Driven Decisions:** Make decisions based on the performance data from A/B tests, optimizing for higher revenue.

Monetization Optimization

1. In-App Purchases (IAP)

- **Pricing Strategy:** Analyze which price points generate the most revenue and consider dynamic pricing models.
- **Promotions:** Create limited-time offers, bundles, and discounts to incentivize IAPs during specific events or milestones.

2. Ads

- **Ad Placements:** Optimize ad placements to maximize user engagement without disrupting the gameplay experience.
- **Ad Mediation:** Use ad mediation platforms to choose the most profitable ad networks for your game.

3. Subscription Models

- **Offer Value:** Ensure that subscription offerings provide substantial value to players, such as exclusive content, currency, or ad-free experiences.
- **Free Trials:** Implement free trial periods to encourage players to subscribe.

4. Virtual Goods

- **Content Updates:** Regularly introduce new virtual goods, skins, or collectibles to keep players interested.
- **Limited-Time Items:** Create a sense of urgency by offering limited-time virtual goods that players can purchase.

5. Incentivized Advertising

- **Rewarded Ads:** Implement rewarded video ads that offer in-game rewards in exchange for watching ads.
- **Offer Walls:** Consider adding offer walls that allow players to earn in-game currency by completing offers from partners.

Data-Driven Decision-Making

1. Regular Analysis

- **Frequency:** Schedule regular data analysis sessions to identify trends and opportunities.
- **Data Visualization:** Use charts, graphs, and dashboards to visualize and comprehend complex revenue data.

2. Feedback Loop

- **Player Feedback:** Pay attention to player feedback regarding monetization and adjust your strategies accordingly.
- **Iterative Approach:** Continuously refine and improve monetization based on player preferences and behavior.

3. Competitor Analysis

- **Market Research:** Study your competitors and analyze their monetization strategies to gain insights.
- **Benchmarks:** Compare your game's performance and monetization metrics to industry benchmarks.

By analyzing revenue data and optimizing your monetization strategies, you can increase your game's profitability while maintaining a positive player experience. Balancing revenue generation with player satisfaction is crucial for long-term success in the gaming industry.

Chapter 17: Legal and Ethical Considerations

Section 17.1: Copyright, Licensing, and Intellectual Property

In the world of game development, understanding and respecting intellectual property rights, copyright, and licensing are critical to avoid legal issues and uphold ethical standards. This section covers key aspects of copyright, licensing, and intellectual property considerations in game development.

1. Copyright Basics

- **What is Copyright?** Copyright is a legal protection granted to the creators of original works, including games, providing exclusive rights to reproduce, distribute, and display the work.
- **Automatic Protection:** In most countries, your game is automatically protected by copyright as soon as it is created and fixed in a tangible medium (e.g., written code or game assets).

2. Fair Use and Transformative Works

- **Fair Use Doctrine:** Understand the concept of fair use, which allows limited use of copyrighted material for purposes such as commentary, criticism, news reporting, and parody.
- **Transformative Works:** Consider how transformative your use of copyrighted material is when assessing whether it falls under fair use.

3. Game Assets and Licensing

- **Asset Licensing:** When using third-party assets (e.g., music, art, or code libraries), respect the terms and conditions specified by their licenses.

- **Open Source Licensing:** Be aware of open source licenses like MIT, GPL, or Apache, and ensure compliance with their requirements.

4. Protecting Your Game

- **Registration:** Consider registering your game with copyright offices or organizations to establish a public record of your ownership.
- **Trademark:** Explore trademark registration for your game's name, logo, or branding elements to protect against infringement.

5. Contracts and Agreements

- **Developer Agreements:** Create clear and comprehensive agreements with team members, contractors, or collaborators, outlining each party's rights and responsibilities.
- **License Agreements:** When licensing your game to publishers or platforms, negotiate agreements that protect your interests and revenue share.

6. Infringement and Enforcement

- **Monitoring:** Continuously monitor your game's distribution channels and online platforms for potential copyright infringement.
- **Enforcement:** Take appropriate legal actions when necessary to protect your intellectual property, such as issuing takedown notices or pursuing legal remedies.

7. Ethical Considerations

- **Respect Others' Work:** Always respect the work and rights of other creators, and seek permission or licensing when using their content.
- **Attribution:** Provide proper attribution for third-party assets used in your game, as required by their licenses.

8. Global Considerations

- **International Copyright Laws:** Be aware that copyright laws vary from one country to another, and international treaties like the Berne Convention may provide additional protections.

9. Seek Legal Counsel

- **Consult Legal Experts:** When in doubt or dealing with complex legal issues, consult with legal experts who specialize in intellectual property and gaming law.

Navigating copyright, licensing, and intellectual property in game development requires careful attention to legal and ethical principles. By respecting the rights of others and protecting your own creative work, you can develop games with confidence, minimize legal risks, and contribute to a fair and thriving gaming industry.

Section 17.2: Privacy Policies and Data Handling

Privacy and data handling are of paramount importance in the digital age, and game developers must adhere to ethical practices and legal requirements when collecting, storing, and using player data. This section explores the key aspects of privacy policies and data handling in the context of game development.

1. **Data Privacy Regulations**

   - **GDPR and CCPA:** Familiarize yourself with major data privacy regulations like the General Data Protection Regulation (GDPR) in Europe and the California Consumer Privacy Act (CCPA) in the United States.
   - **Applicability:** Understand whether your game is subject to these regulations based on factors such as player location and data processing activities.

2. **Privacy Policies**

   - **Necessity:** Create a clear and comprehensive privacy policy that explains how you collect, use, and protect player data.
   - **Transparency:** Ensure transparency in your privacy policy by providing information about data types, purposes, and third-party sharing.
   - **Consent:** Obtain informed and explicit consent from players before collecting their personal data.

3. **Data Collection**

   - **Minimization:** Collect only the data necessary for the intended purpose and avoid excessive or irrelevant data collection.
   - **Sensitive Data:** Exercise caution when dealing with sensitive data, such as personally identifiable information (PII), and implement enhanced security measures.

4. **Data Security**

   - **Encryption:** Implement encryption protocols to protect data during transmission and storage, especially when dealing with sensitive information.
   - **Security Measures:** Employ robust security practices to safeguard against data breaches, including intrusion detection and prevention systems.

5. **User Rights**

   - **Access and Deletion:** Allow players to access their data and request its deletion, as required by data privacy regulations.
   - **Data Portability:** Support data portability, enabling players to transfer their data to other services.

6. **Third-Party Services**

- **Third-Party APIs:** If integrating third-party services (e.g., analytics or advertising networks), ensure they comply with data privacy regulations and align with your privacy policy.
- **Data Sharing:** Clearly disclose any data sharing with third parties in your privacy policy.

7. **Children's Data**

- **COPPA Compliance:** If your game targets children under 13 in the United States, comply with the Children's Online Privacy Protection Act (COPPA) requirements, which include parental consent for data collection.

8. **Data Breach Response**

- **Incident Response Plan:** Develop a data breach incident response plan, outlining steps to take in case of a security incident.
- **Notification:** Comply with legal requirements for notifying affected players and relevant authorities in the event of a data breach.

9. **Testing and Validation**

- **Testing Data Handling:** Test your game thoroughly to ensure that it handles player data securely and accurately.
- **Regular Audits:** Conduct regular privacy audits to assess and improve data handling practices.

10. **Education and Training**

- **Team Awareness:** Ensure that your development team is educated about privacy regulations and data protection principles.
- **Privacy by Design:** Implement a "privacy by design" approach from the beginning of your game development process.

11. **Continuous Compliance**

- **Stay Informed:** Keep up-to-date with evolving data privacy regulations and adjust your practices accordingly.
- **Documentation:** Maintain records of your privacy-related activities, including consent records and data processing procedures.

Respecting player privacy and data protection is not only a legal requirement but also a crucial aspect of maintaining player trust and fostering a positive reputation in the gaming industry. By following best practices and staying informed about data privacy developments, you can navigate the complex landscape of privacy policies and data handling in game development.

Section 17.3: Ethical Considerations in Game Design

Ethical considerations play a significant role in the development of video games. Game developers have a responsibility to create games that are enjoyable, safe, and morally sound. This section explores various ethical aspects that game developers should take into account during the game design process.

1. **Representation and Diversity**

    -   **Inclusivity:** Ensure that your game represents a diverse range of characters, backgrounds, and perspectives. Avoid stereotypes and harmful clichés.
    -   **Cultural Sensitivity:** Be mindful of cultural differences and avoid cultural appropriation or insensitive portrayals.

2. **Content and Themes**

    -   **Age-Appropriateness:** Clearly label and rate your game according to its content, providing appropriate warnings for violence, explicit content, and other potentially distressing themes.
    -   **Mature Themes:** Handle mature themes, such as violence and addiction, with care and responsibility.

3. **Microtransactions and Monetization**

    -   **Transparency:** Clearly communicate the costs and implications of in-game purchases to players.
    -   **Loot Boxes:** Avoid exploitative loot box mechanics that resemble gambling.

4. **Advertising and Promotions**

    -   **Truthfulness:** Ensure that your game's promotional materials accurately represent the actual gameplay and content.
    -   **Deceptive Practices:** Avoid deceptive marketing tactics that mislead players.

5. **Accessibility**

    -   **Inclusive Design:** Make your game accessible to players with disabilities by providing options for customizable controls, subtitles, and other assistive features.
    -   **Testing:** Conduct thorough accessibility testing to identify and address potential barriers.

6. **Player Well-Being**

    -   **Addictive Gameplay:** Be cautious about creating overly addictive mechanics that encourage excessive gameplay and spending.
    -   **Mental Health:** Consider the potential impact of your game on players' mental health and well-being.

7. **Player Data and Privacy**

- **Data Handling:** Handle player data with care, ensuring that it is protected and used responsibly.
- **Informed Consent:** Obtain informed consent from players regarding data collection and sharing practices.

8. **Community and Toxicity**

- **Moderation:** Implement effective moderation systems to combat toxic behavior, hate speech, and harassment within your game's community.
- **Reporting:** Provide easy-to-use reporting tools for players to report abusive behavior.

9. **Storytelling and Narrative Impact**

- **Emotional Impact:** Be aware of the emotional impact your game's narrative may have on players and provide appropriate warnings.
- **Sensitive Topics:** If your game explores sensitive topics like mental health, trauma, or suicide, approach them with sensitivity and provide resources for players.

10. **Real-World Consequences**

- **Consider Consequences:** Reflect on how in-game actions and choices may impact players' real-world attitudes and behaviors.
- **Social Responsibility:** Use your platform to promote positive social messages and contribute to societal betterment.

11. **Testing and Feedback**

- **Player Feedback:** Encourage players to provide feedback on ethical concerns within the game, and take their input seriously.
- **Ethics Committees:** Some game development organizations establish ethics committees to review and address ethical concerns.

12. **Continuous Learning and Improvement**

- **Stay Informed:** Keep up-to-date with discussions and developments in the gaming industry related to ethics and responsible game design.
- **Evolution:** Be willing to adapt and evolve your game's design based on changing ethical standards and player expectations.

By considering these ethical principles and incorporating them into your game design and development process, you can create games that not only entertain but also contribute positively to the gaming community and society at large. Ethical game development is essential for building trust with players and ensuring the long-term success and reputation of your games.

Section 17.4: Accessibility in Games

Accessibility in video games is a critical consideration that ensures that games are playable and enjoyable by a wide range of players, including those with disabilities. Game developers should strive to make their games as inclusive as possible, providing options and features that accommodate different needs and abilities. Here are key aspects of accessibility in games:

1. **Customizable Controls:** Allow players to remap controls to suit their preferences and physical abilities. This is especially important for players with mobility impairments who may require alternative input methods.

2. **Text-to-Speech and Speech-to-Text:** Implement text-to-speech and speech-to-text features to assist players with visual or hearing impairments. This includes providing voiceovers for in-game text and allowing spoken words to be converted into text.

3. **Subtitles and Closed Captions:** Include options for subtitles and closed captions that provide text descriptions of in-game dialogue and sound effects. Ensure that subtitles are customizable in terms of size, color, and background.

4. **Color Blindness Support:** Use color schemes that are friendly to color-blind players. Provide alternative visual cues or patterns for important in-game information that might rely on color differentiation.

5. **Visual and Audio Options:** Allow players to adjust visual settings such as brightness, contrast, and screen shaking. Offer options to adjust audio settings, including volume sliders for different audio channels.

6. **Difficulty Levels:** Implement multiple difficulty levels to cater to players with varying skill levels. Ensure that lower difficulty levels are genuinely accessible and not simply harder modes made easier.

7. **In-Game Tutorials and Hints:** Provide clear and concise tutorials and hints that help players understand the game mechanics and objectives, reducing the learning curve.

8. **Alternative Game Modes:** Create alternative game modes that offer different gameplay experiences. For example, a "no-combat" mode could make the game more accessible to players who struggle with action sequences.

9. **Text Size and Font Options:** Allow players to adjust the size and style of in-game text. Some players may require larger fonts or specific font types for readability.

10. **Sensitivity Settings:** Offer sensitivity settings for input devices like mice and controllers. Players with motor impairments may need slower cursor movement, while others may prefer faster responsiveness.

11. **Button Mashing Alternatives:** Avoid excessive button mashing sequences that can be physically demanding. Allow players alternative ways to accomplish tasks, such as holding a button instead of rapid presses.

12. **Sensory Overload Mitigation:** Provide options to reduce sensory overload by dimming flashing lights, reducing screen shake, or muting intense sound effects.

13. **Testing and Feedback:** Actively involve players with disabilities in the testing process. Seek feedback and make iterative improvements to enhance accessibility.

14. **Accessibility Statements:** Include accessibility statements in your game's documentation or menu screens. Inform players about the available accessibility features and how to enable them.

15. **Legal Compliance:** Be aware of legal requirements related to accessibility, such as the Americans with Disabilities Act (ADA) in the United States and similar legislation in other countries.

Accessibility in games is not only an ethical obligation but also a way to expand your player base and improve the overall gaming experience. By making your games more inclusive, you ensure that everyone, regardless of their abilities, can enjoy and engage with your creations.

Section 17.5: Navigating the Regulatory Landscape

Navigating the regulatory landscape in the context of game development involves understanding and complying with various laws, regulations, and industry standards that govern the creation, distribution, and operation of video games. Compliance with these regulations is essential to avoid legal issues, protect intellectual property, and ensure the ethical and responsible development of games. Here are key aspects of navigating the regulatory landscape in the gaming industry:

1. **Age Ratings and Content Classification:** Different countries have their own rating systems to classify games based on their content and suitability for various age groups. For example, the Entertainment Software Rating Board (ESRB) in the United States and the Pan European Game Information (PEGI) system in Europe. Ensure your game is appropriately rated to inform potential players and comply with legal requirements.

2. **Intellectual Property Rights:** Respect intellectual property laws, including copyrights, trademarks, and patents. Ensure that all content used in your game, including graphics, music, and characters, is either original, properly licensed, or falls under fair use/fair dealing provisions.

3. **Privacy and Data Protection:** Comply with data protection laws, such as the General Data Protection Regulation (GDPR) in Europe. Inform players about data collection and processing practices, obtain consent, and protect user data from breaches.

4. **Online Gambling and Loot Boxes:** Be aware of regulations regarding in-game purchases, loot boxes, and microtransactions. Some jurisdictions consider certain forms of virtual items or gambling mechanics as a form of gambling and may impose restrictions or require licenses.

5. **Consumer Protection:** Ensure that your game does not engage in deceptive practices, false advertising, or unfair treatment of players. Be transparent about in-game purchases and provide clear refund policies.

6. **Accessibility:** As discussed in Section 17.4, ensure that your game complies with accessibility laws and standards, including those related to web content accessibility (WCAG).

7. **Export Control and International Trade:** If your game involves the export or import of technology, consider export control regulations and trade restrictions that may apply. This is especially relevant for games with encryption or military themes.

8. **Local and Regional Regulations:** Be aware of specific regulations and cultural sensitivities in different regions. Some content may be offensive or prohibited in certain countries, and you may need to modify your game accordingly.

9. **Taxation and Revenue Reporting:** Understand tax laws related to game sales, digital goods, and in-game purchases in various jurisdictions. Accurately report revenue and comply with tax obligations.

10. **Network and Platform Compliance:** Comply with platform-specific guidelines and terms of service when publishing on platforms like Steam, Apple App Store, Google Play, or console networks like Xbox Live and PlayStation Network.

11. **Game Mods and User-Generated Content:** If your game supports mods or user-generated content, establish clear policies regarding ownership, licensing, and acceptable content. Be prepared to enforce these policies as necessary.

12. **Legal Consultation:** Seek legal advice from experts in the field of gaming law to ensure compliance with regional and international regulations. Legal counsel can help you draft contracts, negotiate licensing agreements, and address legal issues that may arise during development.

13. **Ethical Considerations:** Beyond legal compliance, consider ethical principles in game design, such as avoiding exploitative mechanics, promoting diversity and inclusion, and addressing social responsibility.

14. **Updates and Maintenance:** Stay informed about regulatory changes and adapt your game accordingly. Regularly update your game to fix compliance-related issues and address emerging legal concerns.

Navigating the regulatory landscape is an ongoing process, and it's crucial to stay informed and adapt to changes in laws and industry standards. By proactively addressing regulatory issues, you can minimize legal risks and build a positive reputation in the gaming industry.

Section 18.1: Crafting an Effective Marketing Strategy

Crafting an effective marketing strategy is a critical component of game development, ensuring that your game reaches its intended audience and achieves success in a competitive market. Your marketing efforts should begin well before your game's release and continue throughout its lifecycle. In this section, we'll explore key elements of crafting a successful marketing strategy for your game.

Understanding Your Target Audience

Before you start marketing your game, it's essential to identify and understand your target audience. This involves creating detailed user personas that describe the characteristics, preferences, and behaviors of your ideal players. Consider factors such as age, gender, interests, gaming platforms, and gaming habits. Tailoring your marketing efforts to a specific audience will make them more effective.

Setting Clear Goals

Define clear and measurable marketing goals for your game. These goals should align with your overall game development objectives. Common marketing goals include building brand awareness, increasing pre-orders or wishlists, growing your social media following, and ultimately driving game sales. Setting specific, achievable goals helps you measure your marketing success.

Building a Strong Online Presence

Establishing a strong online presence is crucial for marketing your game. This includes creating a professional website for your game or studio, setting up social media profiles on platforms relevant to your audience, and maintaining a blog or news section to share updates. Regularly engage with your audience through these channels, share behind-the-scenes content, and build anticipation for your game.

Creating Compelling Game Assets

High-quality visuals and engaging content are essential for capturing the attention of potential players. Invest in creating compelling game assets, including screenshots, gameplay videos, and promotional artwork. These assets should effectively convey your game's unique selling points and appeal to your target audience.

Leveraging Social Media and Influencers

Utilize social media platforms to connect with your audience and generate buzz around your game. Engage in conversations, respond to comments, and run targeted advertising campaigns. Collaborate with influencers and content creators who align with your game's genre and audience to reach a broader player base.

Implementing Email Marketing

Email marketing is a powerful tool for nurturing your community and keeping players informed. Build an email list by offering incentives such as exclusive content or early access. Send regular newsletters with updates, developer insights, and promotional offers to keep your audience engaged.

Pre-launch Marketing

A successful pre-launch marketing campaign can significantly impact your game's success. Consider strategies such as running closed beta tests, offering pre-order incentives, and creating teaser trailers. Generate excitement and anticipation to build a strong player base before your game's release.

Post-launch Support and Community Engagement

Marketing doesn't end at launch; it continues throughout your game's lifecycle. Provide ongoing support and updates to keep players engaged and address issues promptly. Foster a sense of community through forums, social media groups, and regular interactions with players.

Measuring and Analyzing Results

Regularly analyze the effectiveness of your marketing efforts by tracking key performance indicators (KPIs) such as website traffic, social media engagement, conversion rates, and game sales. Use these insights to adjust your strategy and optimize your marketing campaigns.

Adapting to Player Feedback

Listen to player feedback and adapt your marketing strategy accordingly. Address concerns, implement player-requested features, and maintain transparency in your communication. Positive player experiences can lead to word-of-mouth marketing and brand loyalty.

In conclusion, crafting an effective marketing strategy for your game is essential for its success in a competitive industry. By understanding your target audience, setting clear goals, building a strong online presence, creating compelling game assets, and engaging with your community, you can maximize your game's visibility and drive player interest.

Marketing should be an ongoing and adaptive process that evolves with your game's lifecycle.

Section 18.2: Building a Press Kit and Reaching Out to Media

Building a press kit and effectively reaching out to media outlets is a crucial part of your game's marketing strategy. A well-organized press kit provides journalists and influencers with the information and assets they need to cover your game accurately. In this section, we'll explore the key elements of creating a press kit and strategies for reaching out to the media.

Building Your Press Kit

1. Overview Document

Start your press kit with an overview document that provides a brief introduction to your game. Include the game's title, genre, platform(s), release date, and a concise description of its key features and unique selling points.

2. Press Release

Craft a well-written press release that highlights important news or updates about your game. This could include announcements like launch dates, major updates, partnerships, or significant milestones.

3. Game Information

Include detailed information about your game, such as its storyline, gameplay mechanics, and objectives. Provide context and background that helps journalists understand the game's world and purpose.

4. Screenshots and Gameplay Videos

Include high-resolution screenshots and gameplay videos that showcase different aspects of your game. Ensure that these assets are visually appealing and accurately represent the game's graphics and gameplay.

5. Artwork and Logos

Share promotional artwork, including the game's logo and key art. These visuals should be suitable for use in articles, reviews, and promotional materials.

6. Developer Background

Include information about your development team, studio, and their previous work. Highlight any notable achievements, awards, or industry recognition.

7. Contact Information

Provide clear and easily accessible contact information for media inquiries. Include an email address and phone number where journalists can reach you for interviews or additional information.

Reaching Out to Media

1. Research and Targeting

Research media outlets, websites, and journalists that cover games similar to yours. Target outlets that align with your game's genre and audience. Make a list of potential contacts.

2. Personalized Pitches

Craft personalized pitches when reaching out to media. Mention specific articles or content they've covered in the past that relate to your game. Explain why your game would be of interest to their audience.

3. Email Outreach

Send concise and professional email pitches to your list of media contacts. Use a compelling subject line that grabs their attention. Attach your press kit or provide a link to download it.

4. Press Release Distribution Services

Consider using press release distribution services to reach a broader audience. These services can help you distribute your press releases to various media outlets and industry contacts.

5. Follow-Up

Don't hesitate to follow up with journalists if you don't receive a response initially. Politely remind them of your pitch and offer additional information or assets if needed.

6. Be Available for Interviews

Be prepared to respond to interview requests promptly. Make yourself available for interviews, podcasts, or video features to provide insights into your game's development and story.

7. Social Media Engagement

Engage with journalists and media outlets on social media platforms. Share their coverage of your game and express gratitude for their support. Building relationships with media professionals can lead to long-term partnerships.

If possible, attend gaming events, conferences, and conventions to network with journalists and influencers in person. These events offer valuable opportunities to showcase your game and make direct connections.

In summary, creating a comprehensive press kit and effectively reaching out to media outlets can significantly enhance your game's visibility and coverage. Personalization, professionalism, and engagement are key when interacting with journalists and influencers. Building strong relationships with the media can lead to extensive coverage and positive exposure for your game.

Section 18.3: Leveraging Social Media for Promotion

Social media has become an integral part of game marketing and promotion. It offers a powerful platform to engage with your audience, build anticipation for your game, and create a community of dedicated fans. In this section, we'll explore strategies for leveraging social media effectively to promote your game.

Choosing the Right Social Media Platforms

Not all social media platforms are created equal, and each has its own strengths and audience demographics. It's essential to choose the platforms that align with your game's target audience and genre. Here are some popular social media platforms and their characteristics:

1. Twitter
- Ideal for short and frequent updates.
- Great for engaging with your community and sharing news.
- Effective for using hashtags to increase visibility.

2. Facebook
- Suitable for longer-form posts and multimedia content.
- Offers the ability to create a dedicated page for your game.
- Allows for targeted advertising and promotion.

3. Instagram
- Focuses on visual content, including images and short videos.
- Effective for showcasing game art, character designs, and gameplay snippets.
- Utilizes hashtags for discoverability.

4. TikTok
- Well-suited for short and entertaining videos.
- Particularly popular among younger audiences.

- Viral challenges and trends can boost visibility.

5. YouTube
- Ideal for hosting trailers, gameplay videos, and developer diaries.
- Offers a platform for in-depth content and tutorials.
- Provides opportunities for monetization.

6. Discord
- Excellent for building a community of players and fans.
- Offers text and voice chat channels for real-time engagement.
- Allows for direct interaction with your audience.

Creating Engaging Content

Once you've selected the appropriate social media platforms, focus on creating engaging and shareable content. Here are some content ideas:

1. Teasers and Trailers
- Share teaser videos and trailers that create excitement and intrigue about your game.
- Use eye-catching visuals and compelling storytelling.

2. Behind-the-Scenes
- Offer a glimpse into your development process with behind-the-scenes content.
- Share concept art, design decisions, and developer stories.

3. Developer Diaries
- Create a series of developer diaries that detail various aspects of your game's development.
- Discuss challenges, successes, and lessons learned.

4. Artwork and Screenshots
- Share high-quality artwork, character designs, and in-game screenshots.
- Highlight the visual appeal of your game.

5. Interactive Content
- Engage your audience with interactive content like polls, quizzes, and challenges.
- Encourage user-generated content and fan art.

Consistency and Engagement

Consistency is key to maintaining an active and growing social media presence. Develop a posting schedule and stick to it. Interact with your audience by responding to comments, messages, and mentions promptly. Encourage discussions and conversations related to your game.

Hashtags and Trends

Utilize relevant hashtags and follow industry trends to increase the visibility of your posts. Participate in trending challenges or topics that align with your game to reach a broader audience.

Paid Promotion

Consider allocating a budget for paid promotion on social media platforms. Targeted advertising can help you reach specific demographics and expand your game's reach.

Analytics and Insights

Regularly analyze the performance of your social media efforts using platform-specific analytics tools. Monitor engagement metrics, follower growth, and the effectiveness of your posts. Use these insights to refine your social media strategy.

In summary, social media is a potent tool for promoting your game and connecting with your audience. By choosing the right platforms, creating engaging content, maintaining consistency, and utilizing trends and analytics, you can build a strong social media presence that enhances your game's visibility and success.

Section 18.4: Participating in Gaming Conferences and Expos

Participating in gaming conferences and expos is a crucial element of marketing and promoting your game. These events provide an opportunity to showcase your game to a wider audience, connect with industry professionals, and gather feedback from players and peers. In this section, we'll explore how to make the most of gaming conferences and expos.

Choosing the Right Events

There are numerous gaming conferences and expos held globally, each catering to different aspects of the gaming industry. When deciding which events to attend, consider your game's genre, target audience, and development stage. Here are some renowned gaming events:

1. E3 (Electronic Entertainment Expo)
- One of the largest gaming expos globally, featuring major game announcements and industry leaders.
- Ideal for high-profile game launches and AAA titles.

2. PAX (Penny Arcade Expo)
- Includes multiple regional events like PAX West, PAX East, and PAX South.
- Known for a focus on indie games and community engagement.

3. GDC (Game Developers Conference)
- A gathering of game developers, industry professionals, and educators.
- Offers networking opportunities and in-depth sessions on game development.

4. Gamescom
- Europe's largest gaming event, attracting developers, publishers, and fans.
- Suitable for both AAA and indie game showcases.

5. IndieCade
- Dedicated to celebrating and promoting indie games and developers.
- Emphasizes innovation and creativity in game design.

6. EGX (Eurogamer Expo)
- The UK's largest gaming event, featuring a diverse range of games and platforms.
- Ideal for showcasing games in the European market.

7. Tokyo Game Show
- A major event for the Asian gaming market, featuring Japanese and international games.
- Opportunities for networking with Asian publishers and developers.

Preparing for Conferences and Expos

Once you've chosen the right event for your game, thorough preparation is essential for a successful showcase:

1. Build an Engaging Booth
- Design an eye-catching booth that reflects your game's theme and captures attention.
- Include demo stations, promotional materials, and engaging visuals.

2. Develop a Compelling Pitch
- Prepare a concise and compelling pitch to introduce your game to attendees.
- Highlight unique features and gameplay elements.

3. Create Marketing Materials
- Design brochures, posters, and business cards to distribute to interested parties.
- Ensure these materials are visually appealing and informative.

4. Test and Polish Your Game
- Before the event, thoroughly test your game to eliminate bugs and glitches.
- Provide a stable and enjoyable experience for players.

5. Staff Your Booth
- Ensure you have a dedicated team to manage your booth and engage with visitors.
- Train your team to answer questions and interact professionally.

Networking and Feedback

Gaming conferences and expos offer invaluable networking opportunities. Engage with fellow developers, publishers, and players to establish connections and gather feedback:

1. Networking Events
- Attend industry parties, mixers, and meetups to connect with professionals.
- Exchange ideas, collaborate on projects, and explore partnerships.

2. Playtesting and Feedback
- Encourage attendees to playtest your game and provide feedback.
- Gather valuable insights to improve your game before release.

3. Press and Media
- Reach out to gaming journalists and influencers to schedule interviews or demos.
- Generate media coverage and build anticipation for your game.

Post-Event Follow-Up

After the conference or expo concludes, don't forget the importance of post-event follow-up:

1. Thank-You Emails
- Send thank-you emails to everyone who visited your booth or expressed interest.
- Maintain relationships and express gratitude for their support.

2. Analysis and Improvement
- Analyze the feedback and data gathered during the event.
- Use insights to refine your game and marketing strategy.

3. Stay Connected
- Stay in touch with the contacts you made during the event.
- Networking is an ongoing process, and maintaining connections is essential.

In summary, participating in gaming conferences and expos can significantly boost your game's visibility and success. By carefully selecting events, preparing your showcase, networking effectively, and following up after the event, you can maximize the impact of your presence at these industry gatherings.

Section 18.5: Publishing on Different Platforms and Stores

Publishing your game on various platforms and app stores is a crucial step toward reaching a wider audience and generating revenue. Each platform and store has its own requirements, guidelines, and potential benefits. In this section, we'll explore the process of publishing your game on different platforms and app stores.

1. PC and Console Platforms

Steam

Steam is one of the largest digital distribution platforms for PC gaming. To publish your game on Steam, you'll need to go through the Steam Direct program, pay a fee, and meet certain quality standards. Steam provides a vast audience, a built-in community, and access to various features like Steam Workshop for user-generated content.

Epic Games Store

Epic Games Store is another prominent PC gaming platform. Epic offers attractive revenue share options for developers, and they often feature games for free as part of their weekly giveaways. To publish on the Epic Games Store, you can submit your game through their developer portal.

Xbox and PlayStation

For console game development, Microsoft's Xbox and Sony's PlayStation offer development programs. You'll need access to their development kits and may need to go through a certification process. Once approved, your game can be published on their respective platforms, Xbox Live and PlayStation Network.

2. Mobile Platforms

Apple App Store

To publish your game on iOS devices, you'll need to enroll in the Apple Developer Program. This program allows you to submit your game to the App Store. Be prepared to adhere to Apple's strict guidelines for quality, security, and content.

Google Play Store

For Android devices, the Google Play Store is the primary distribution platform. Publishing on Google Play involves registering as a developer, creating a developer account, and submitting your game. Google also provides tools for beta testing and gradual rollouts.

3. Web and Browser Games

HTML5/WebGL

Publishing web-based games is relatively simple. You can host your game on your website or use platforms like Itch.io or GameJolt to reach a broader audience. Ensure your game is optimized for web performance, and consider implementing monetization options like ads or donations.

Facebook Instant Games

Facebook offers a platform for publishing instant games that can be played directly on the Facebook platform. You'll need to join the Facebook for Developers program and adhere to their guidelines.

4. VR and AR Platforms

Oculus Store

For virtual reality (VR) games on Oculus devices, you can publish your game on the Oculus Store. Oculus provides developer resources and support for VR game development.

Apple ARKit and Google ARCore

If you're developing augmented reality (AR) games, consider publishing on platforms like Apple's ARKit for iOS and Google's ARCore for Android. These platforms allow you to create immersive AR experiences.

5. Cross-Platform Game Engines

Many game engines, such as Unity and Unreal Engine, support multi-platform development. Using these engines, you can create games that can be easily exported and published on various platforms simultaneously. This approach can save time and resources.

6. Distribution and Monetization Strategies

Once your game is published, you'll need to consider distribution and monetization strategies. These may include pricing your game, offering in-app purchases, implementing ads, or using subscription models. It's essential to analyze the preferences of your target audience and adapt your monetization strategy accordingly.

7. Post-Launch Maintenance

After your game is published, the work isn't over. You'll need to provide updates, fix bugs, and address player feedback to maintain a positive reputation and keep players engaged. Regularly monitoring your game's performance and implementing improvements is key to long-term success.

In conclusion, publishing your game on different platforms and app stores requires careful planning and adherence to platform-specific guidelines. Each platform offers unique advantages and challenges, so it's essential to choose the ones that align with your game's target audience and development capabilities. By effectively publishing and promoting your game, you can maximize its visibility and potential for success in the competitive gaming market.

Chapter 19: Future Trends in JavaScript Gaming

In this chapter, we'll explore the exciting future trends in JavaScript gaming. The world of game development is constantly evolving, driven by emerging technologies and changing player expectations. Staying ahead of the curve is essential for game developers to create innovative and engaging gaming experiences. Let's delve into some of the future trends that are likely to shape the landscape of JavaScript gaming in the coming years.

Section 19.1: Emerging Technologies and Their Impact

As technology continues to advance, several emerging trends will significantly impact JavaScript gaming. Let's take a closer look at these trends:

1. WebAssembly (Wasm)

WebAssembly is a binary instruction format that enables high-performance execution of code on web browsers. It allows developers to write games in languages like C++ and Rust and compile them to run directly in the browser. This technology offers near-native performance and opens up new possibilities for complex, resource-intensive games in JavaScript.

2. WebXR and Immersive Experiences

WebXR, an extension of WebVR, allows developers to create immersive virtual and augmented reality experiences directly in the browser. With the growing popularity of VR and AR, integrating WebXR into JavaScript games will provide players with truly immersive gameplay.

3. Progressive Web Apps (PWAs)

PWAs are web applications that offer a native app-like experience while being accessible through web browsers. JavaScript game developers can leverage PWAs to reach a broader audience, enhance user engagement, and provide offline access to games.

4. 5G and Cloud Gaming

The rollout of 5G networks and the rise of cloud gaming services will enable players to stream resource-intensive games seamlessly. JavaScript game developers can tap into this trend by creating games that harness the power of cloud servers, allowing players to enjoy high-quality gaming experiences on a variety of devices.

5. Machine Learning and AI

Machine learning and artificial intelligence (AI) are becoming increasingly important in game development. JavaScript developers can incorporate AI-driven features like intelligent NPCs, dynamic content generation, and personalized gameplay experiences to make games more engaging and responsive.

6. Blockchain and NFTs

Blockchain technology and non-fungible tokens (NFTs) are gaining traction in the gaming industry. Developers can use blockchain to create unique in-game assets, provably rare items, and player-driven economies. Integrating blockchain into JavaScript games can enhance player ownership and trading possibilities.

7. Cross-Platform Development

Cross-platform development tools and frameworks will continue to evolve, making it easier for developers to create games for multiple platforms with a single codebase. This trend reduces development time and enables games to reach wider audiences.

8. Accessibility and Inclusivity

Developers are increasingly recognizing the importance of making games accessible to players with disabilities. JavaScript game development will see more efforts to ensure games are inclusive and can be enjoyed by everyone.

9. Sustainability and Eco-Friendly Gaming

As environmental concerns grow, there will be a push toward eco-friendly gaming practices. JavaScript game developers will explore ways to reduce energy consumption and minimize the carbon footprint of online gaming.

In conclusion, the future of JavaScript gaming holds exciting prospects, driven by innovative technologies and evolving player preferences. Staying informed about these trends and adapting to the changing landscape will be essential for developers looking to create successful and relevant games in the years to come. As JavaScript continues to evolve and mature, it will remain a versatile and powerful tool for crafting captivating gaming experiences.

Section 19.2: Virtual Reality (VR) and Augmented Reality (AR) in Web Games

Virtual Reality (VR) and Augmented Reality (AR) have been gaining momentum in the gaming industry, and their integration with web games using JavaScript is a promising trend. These technologies offer immersive experiences that can elevate gameplay to new levels. Let's explore how VR and AR are shaping the future of web-based games.

VR and AR: What's the Difference?

Before delving into their impact on web games, it's essential to distinguish between VR and AR:

- **Virtual Reality (VR):** VR immerses players in a completely virtual environment, shutting out the physical world. Players typically wear VR headsets that provide a

223

360-degree view of a digital world. This technology is perfect for creating entirely fictional game worlds.

- **Augmented Reality (AR):** AR, on the other hand, blends digital elements with the real world. Players view the real world through a device like a smartphone or AR glasses, and digital content is overlaid onto their surroundings. AR is excellent for enhancing real-world experiences with game elements.

Web-Based VR Games

Web-based VR games are becoming increasingly accessible thanks to technologies like WebVR and WebXR. These frameworks allow developers to create VR experiences that users can access directly through their web browsers, eliminating the need for specialized VR hardware or app installations.

Developers can leverage JavaScript to build VR games that cater to a wide audience. With JavaScript's versatility, game logic, user interactions, and immersive VR experiences can be crafted seamlessly. Libraries like A-Frame make it easier to create VR content using HTML and JavaScript.

Augmented Reality on the Web

Augmented Reality is finding its way into web-based games as well. WebAR APIs enable developers to create AR experiences that users can access through web browsers, making it more accessible than ever. JavaScript plays a central role in building interactive and dynamic AR content.

AR games on the web can range from location-based games that use GPS data to overlay digital elements onto the real world to educational games that provide interactive learning experiences. JavaScript frameworks and libraries facilitate the integration of AR features, making it easier for developers to experiment with this exciting technology.

Cross-Platform Compatibility

One of the significant advantages of using JavaScript for VR and AR web games is cross-platform compatibility. Since JavaScript runs in web browsers, players can access VR and AR experiences on various devices, including smartphones, tablets, desktops, and even VR headsets.

This cross-platform nature ensures a broader reach for web-based VR and AR games, allowing developers to target a diverse audience. It also simplifies distribution since players don't need to install dedicated apps, reducing friction and improving accessibility.

Challenges and Considerations

While the integration of VR and AR in web games is promising, it comes with challenges. VR experiences demand high-performance graphics and low latency, which can be challenging to achieve in web browsers. Developers must optimize their code, assets, and rendering techniques to ensure a smooth VR experience.

For AR, ensuring accurate real-world tracking and object recognition can be complex, especially when relying on web technologies. Device compatibility and browser support for AR features can also be limiting factors.

Conclusion

The future of web-based gaming looks increasingly immersive and interactive, thanks to the integration of VR and AR technologies. JavaScript's role in building these experiences cannot be understated, as it enables developers to create captivating VR and AR games that can be accessed by a broad range of users. As these technologies continue to mature, we can expect to see more innovative and engaging web-based VR and AR games in the coming years.

Section 19.3: The Role of AI in Future Game Development

Artificial Intelligence (AI) is poised to play a transformative role in the future of game development. As technology advances, AI's capabilities are expanding, opening up new possibilities for creating immersive and engaging gaming experiences. In this section, we'll explore the evolving role of AI in the gaming industry and how it can shape the future of game development.

AI-Powered Game Design

AI is becoming increasingly involved in the game design process. Game designers can leverage AI algorithms to generate content, such as levels, characters, and even entire game worlds. Procedural content generation, driven by AI, allows for the creation of vast and dynamic gaming environments that adapt to player actions.

For example, AI can generate randomized dungeon layouts in a role-playing game or design challenging puzzles in a puzzle platformer. By automating content creation, developers can reduce the time and effort required to build complex game worlds, ultimately leading to more diverse and engaging gameplay experiences.

Enhanced Non-Player Characters (NPCs)

AI-driven NPCs are central to creating lifelike and challenging gaming experiences. In the future, we can expect NPCs to exhibit more advanced behaviors, making interactions with them feel more natural and immersive. AI can enable NPCs to adapt to player actions, learn from their behavior, and even simulate emotions and personalities.

For instance, in a role-playing game, AI-controlled NPCs could remember past interactions with the player and develop unique responses and relationships over time. This level of sophistication in NPC behavior can lead to more compelling storytelling and gameplay dynamics.

Smarter Adversarial Agents

AI is also revolutionizing how adversarial agents, such as enemy characters or opponents, behave in games. Advanced AI algorithms can create opponents that challenge players' skills and adapt to their strategies. This ensures that the gaming experience remains engaging and avoids becoming predictable.

In competitive multiplayer games, AI can be used to create intelligent matchmaking systems that pair players with opponents of similar skill levels, ensuring fair and exciting matches. Moreover, AI can detect and prevent cheating behaviors, enhancing the overall integrity of online gaming.

Dynamic Storytelling

The future of game narratives is likely to be heavily influenced by AI. Dynamic storytelling systems powered by AI can adjust the game's plot, dialogue, and outcomes based on player choices and actions. This creates a personalized and evolving narrative that responds to the player's decisions.

Imagine playing a role-playing game where your choices not only impact the story's progression but also shape the world and the relationships between characters. AI can analyze player decisions in real-time and adapt the narrative to deliver a truly unique storytelling experience.

AI-Driven Game Testing and Balancing

AI can also play a critical role in game development processes such as testing and balancing. AI-driven bots can simulate player behavior and thoroughly test various aspects of a game, identifying bugs, performance issues, and balance problems more efficiently than human testers.

Furthermore, AI algorithms can analyze player data to fine-tune game balance. They can adjust difficulty levels, rewards, and pacing to ensure that the game provides an enjoyable and fair experience for players of all skill levels.

Ethical Considerations

As AI becomes more integrated into game development, ethical considerations arise. Developers must be conscious of potential biases in AI algorithms and ensure that AI-driven NPCs, storytelling, and matchmaking systems are designed to be inclusive and fair. Additionally, AI-generated content must meet ethical standards, avoiding harmful or offensive elements.

In conclusion, AI is poised to revolutionize the gaming industry, offering new avenues for creativity, immersion, and player engagement. As AI technologies continue to advance, game developers will have the tools to create more dynamic, responsive, and compelling gaming experiences that cater to a diverse and evolving player base. However, it is crucial to approach AI integration in games with ethical considerations and a commitment to providing inclusive and enjoyable experiences for all players.

Section 19.4: Blockchain and Cryptocurrency in Games

Blockchain technology and cryptocurrency are gaining traction in the gaming industry, offering unique opportunities and challenges for both game developers and players. In this section, we'll delve into the integration of blockchain and cryptocurrency into games and explore their potential impact on the future of gaming.

Blockchain in Gaming

1. Ownership and Digital Assets

Blockchain's primary value proposition in gaming lies in its ability to establish true ownership of in-game assets. Traditionally, players have limited control over their virtual items, which are stored on centralized servers and can be subject to censorship or loss if a game shuts down. With blockchain, these assets are recorded as non-fungible tokens (NFTs), providing players with verifiable ownership.

Developers can create NFTs for in-game items, characters, or land, allowing players to buy, sell, and trade them across different games or platforms. This interoperability can lead to a more open and player-centric gaming ecosystem.

2. Transparency and Fair Play

Blockchain's transparent and tamper-resistant nature can address issues related to cheating, fraud, and unfair gameplay. Smart contracts, self-executing agreements on the blockchain, can govern game rules and ensure fairness. For example, smart contracts can verify the rarity of in-game items or enforce the rules of a decentralized tournament.

3. Decentralized Games

Blockchain enables the development of decentralized games, where game logic and assets are distributed across a network of nodes, making it difficult for any single entity to control or manipulate the game. These games often use blockchain-based tokens as a form of currency, offering players true ownership and control of their in-game assets.

Cryptocurrency Integration

1. In-Game Economies

Cryptocurrency, such as Bitcoin or Ethereum, can be integrated into games as a means of in-game currency. Players can earn, spend, or trade cryptocurrency within the game environment. This introduces real economic value to in-game actions and can incentivize player engagement.

2. Microtransactions and Payments

Cryptocurrency can streamline microtransactions within games. Players can make small payments or purchases without the need for traditional payment methods, reducing friction in the purchasing process. Additionally, cryptocurrency transactions are often faster and more secure than traditional methods.

3. Play-to-Earn Models

Some games have embraced "play-to-earn" models, where players can earn cryptocurrency by playing the game and achieving in-game goals. This has the potential to transform gaming into a source of income for skilled players, especially in regions where economic opportunities are limited.

Challenges and Considerations

While blockchain and cryptocurrency offer exciting possibilities, they also present challenges and considerations:

1. Scalability and Performance

Blockchain networks, particularly public ones like Ethereum, face scalability and performance issues, such as high transaction costs and slow confirmation times. Game developers need to choose appropriate blockchain platforms and solutions to mitigate these challenges.

2. Regulatory and Legal Compliance

The regulatory landscape for cryptocurrency and blockchain in gaming is evolving. Developers must navigate legal and compliance issues, such as taxation, anti-money laundering (AML) regulations, and consumer protection laws.

3. Environmental Concerns

The energy-intensive nature of some blockchain networks, like proof-of-work (PoW) chains, has raised environmental concerns. Game developers may opt for eco-friendly blockchain solutions or consider the environmental impact when making integration decisions.

4. Player Education

Players need to understand blockchain and cryptocurrency concepts to fully benefit from their integration into games. Developers should provide user-friendly interfaces and educational resources to onboard players.

The Future of Blockchain and Cryptocurrency in Games

As blockchain technology matures and cryptocurrency adoption grows, their presence in the gaming industry is likely to expand. Developers who embrace these technologies have the potential to create innovative and player-centric experiences, while players can enjoy true ownership of in-game assets and new economic opportunities. However, careful consideration of technical, legal, and ethical aspects is crucial to ensuring the successful integration of blockchain and cryptocurrency into the gaming ecosystem.

Section 19.5: Predictions for the Next Decade of JavaScript Gaming

The future of JavaScript gaming holds exciting possibilities as technology continues to advance. In this section, we'll explore some predictions for the next decade of JavaScript gaming and the trends that may shape the industry.

1. WebAssembly for High-Performance Games

WebAssembly (Wasm) is poised to play a significant role in improving the performance of JavaScript games. By allowing code written in languages like C++ and Rust to run at near-native speed in web browsers, Wasm opens the door to more complex and resource-intensive games. As browsers and tooling for WebAssembly continue to evolve, we can expect to see a surge in high-performance JavaScript games.

2. Increased Adoption of 3D and VR Gaming

JavaScript-powered 3D games and virtual reality (VR) experiences are likely to become more prevalent. With the availability of WebGL for 3D graphics and emerging WebXR standards for VR and augmented reality (AR), developers can create immersive gaming experiences that run directly in web browsers. As hardware becomes more accessible and affordable, 3D and VR gaming will extend to a broader audience.

3. Progressive Web Apps (PWAs) for Gaming

Progressive Web Apps (PWAs) offer a seamless and cross-platform gaming experience. These web applications can be installed on users' devices and offer offline functionality, making them ideal for mobile and desktop gaming. Expect to see more JavaScript games adopting PWA technology to provide instant access and improved user engagement.

4. AI and Procedural Content Generation

Artificial intelligence (AI) will play a more prominent role in JavaScript gaming, enabling smarter NPCs, dynamic storytelling, and adaptive gameplay. Procedural content generation will also become more sophisticated, allowing games to create diverse and unique experiences for players. AI-driven game design tools will assist developers in creating rich and dynamic game worlds.

5. Cloud Gaming and Streaming Services

Cloud gaming services like Google Stadia and Microsoft's Project xCloud are pushing the boundaries of where and how games can be played. JavaScript game developers may explore cloud-based gaming solutions, leveraging the power of server-side rendering and high-performance hardware. This trend will enable more demanding games to run on a wider range of devices.

6. Cross-Platform Development

Cross-platform development tools and frameworks will continue to evolve, making it easier for developers to create games that run seamlessly on multiple platforms, including web browsers, mobile devices, and consoles. JavaScript, with its wide compatibility, will remain a vital language for cross-platform gaming.

7. NFT Integration and Ownership

The integration of non-fungible tokens (NFTs) and blockchain technology in JavaScript games may deepen, allowing players to truly own in-game assets. Developers will explore innovative ways to use NFTs for items, characters, and even in-game achievements, providing players with a sense of ownership and scarcity.

8. Enhanced Game Analytics and Personalization

As data analytics tools become more sophisticated, game developers will gain deeper insights into player behavior and preferences. This data will fuel personalized gaming experiences, tailoring gameplay, storylines, and in-game content to individual players' preferences.

9. Increased Focus on Accessibility and Inclusivity

Game developers will continue to prioritize accessibility and inclusivity in game design. JavaScript games will feature more customizable controls, visual aids, and options for players with disabilities, ensuring that gaming remains an inclusive pastime for all.

10. Sustainable Game Development Practices

Sustainability will be a growing concern in game development. Developers will adopt eco-friendly practices, including optimizing code for energy efficiency and using environmentally friendly hosting solutions. Players may also see more games with environmental themes and messages.

In conclusion, JavaScript gaming is poised for a dynamic and innovative future. With advancements in technology, tools, and player expectations, the next decade promises to bring new and exciting gaming experiences to audiences worldwide. Developers who stay agile and adapt to these emerging trends will be at the forefront of shaping the future of JavaScript gaming.

Chapter 20: Building a Portfolio and Career in Game Development

Section 20.1: Creating a Compelling Game Development Portfolio

A strong portfolio is a crucial asset for anyone aspiring to start or advance their career in game development. Whether you're a seasoned developer looking for new opportunities or a fresh graduate aiming to land your first job, an impressive portfolio can make a significant difference. In this section, we'll explore the essential elements of creating a compelling game development portfolio.

1. Showcase Your Best Work

Your portfolio should highlight your best and most impressive projects. Select a range of games that demonstrate your skills, creativity, and versatility as a developer. Include both completed games and works in progress, if they showcase your potential.

2. Provide Clear Project Descriptions

For each project, provide clear and concise descriptions. Explain the concept, objectives, and any unique features of the game. Mention the technologies and tools you used, such as JavaScript libraries or frameworks, to give prospective employers or collaborators insight into your expertise.

3. Include Playable Demos

Whenever possible, include playable demos or links to your games. This allows visitors to interact with your work and experience your games firsthand. It's a powerful way to demonstrate your abilities and engage potential employers or collaborators.

4. Showcase Different Skills

Your portfolio should showcase a variety of skills relevant to game development. This might include coding, graphics design, sound design, level design, and gameplay mechanics. Highlighting your diverse skill set can make you more attractive to potential employers or teams.

5. Document Your Process

Consider documenting your development process for some of your projects. This could involve creating development diaries, writing blog posts, or sharing insights on social media. Sharing your journey and challenges can demonstrate your dedication and passion for game development.

6. Collaborative Projects

If you've worked on collaborative projects, make sure to credit your team members appropriately. Highlighting your ability to work effectively in a team is valuable for demonstrating your professionalism.

7. Keep It Updated

Regularly update your portfolio with new projects and improvements to existing ones. An outdated portfolio may not reflect your current skills and abilities. Keep it fresh to stay competitive in the job market.

8. Responsive Design

Ensure that your portfolio website is mobile-friendly and responsive. Many employers and recruiters browse portfolios on various devices, so a responsive design is essential for a seamless user experience.

9. Personalize Your Portfolio

Consider adding a personal touch to your portfolio by sharing your story, inspirations, and what drives your passion for game development. Humanizing your portfolio can make you more relatable to potential employers.

10. Seek Feedback

Before finalizing your portfolio, seek feedback from peers, mentors, or industry professionals. Constructive criticism can help you identify areas for improvement and make your portfolio more compelling.

In conclusion, your game development portfolio is a reflection of your skills, creativity, and potential. A well-crafted portfolio can open doors to exciting opportunities in the gaming industry. Invest time and effort into creating a compelling portfolio that sets you apart and showcases your unique abilities as a game developer.

Section 20.2: Freelancing and Contract Work in Game Development

Freelancing and contract work are viable career paths in the game development industry, offering flexibility, diverse experiences, and the potential for substantial income. In this section, we'll delve into the world of freelancing and contracting, discussing how to get started, find clients, and succeed in this dynamic field.

1. Getting Started as a Freelancer

To begin your journey as a freelance game developer, it's essential to have a strong skill set and a portfolio that showcases your abilities. Clients are more likely to hire freelancers with a proven track record of delivering high-quality work. Ensure that your portfolio includes a variety of game development projects to attract different types of clients.

2. Building an Online Presence

Establishing an online presence is crucial for freelancers. Create a professional website or portfolio to showcase your work and provide contact information. Utilize social media platforms like LinkedIn, Twitter, and professional forums to connect with potential clients and other freelancers.

3. Networking

Networking is a fundamental aspect of freelancing success. Attend game development conferences, seminars, and industry events to meet potential clients and collaborators. Join online communities, such as game development forums and LinkedIn groups, to expand your network.

4. Platforms for Finding Freelance Opportunities

Several online platforms connect freelancers with clients seeking game development services. Some popular platforms include Upwork, Freelancer, Toptal, and Fiverr. Create a compelling profile on these platforms and actively bid on relevant projects.

5. Freelance Specializations

Consider specializing in a particular niche within game development, such as mobile game development, VR/AR game development, or indie game development. Specialization can help you stand out and attract clients seeking expertise in a specific area.

6. Setting Your Rates

Determining your freelance rates can be challenging. Research industry standards and consider factors such as your skill level, experience, project complexity, and market demand. Be transparent with clients about your pricing structure.

7. Contracts and Agreements

Always use written contracts or agreements when working with clients. Clearly define project scope, deliverables, timelines, payment terms, and any revisions. Contracts protect both you and your clients and ensure a smooth working relationship.

8. Time Management

Effective time management is essential for freelancers. Set realistic deadlines and milestones for your projects. Use project management tools and calendars to stay organized and meet client expectations.

9. Managing Finances

As a freelancer, you are responsible for managing your finances, including taxes, invoicing, and expenses. Consider consulting with an accountant or using accounting software to stay on top of your financial obligations.

10. Building Client Relationships

Building strong relationships with clients can lead to repeat business and referrals. Communicate effectively, provide regular project updates, and be responsive to client feedback and concerns.

11. Handling Challenges

Freelancing may come with challenges, such as irregular income and the need for self-discipline. Prepare for these challenges by establishing a financial cushion and developing a structured work routine.

12. Expanding Your Freelance Career

As you gain experience and recognition, you can expand your freelance career by taking on larger projects, collaborating with other freelancers or agencies, and exploring new niches within game development.

In conclusion, freelancing and contract work offer game developers the opportunity to work on exciting projects, gain diverse experiences, and achieve financial independence. Building a successful freelance career requires a combination of skills, networking, effective communication, and adaptability. With dedication and a strong work ethic, freelancers can thrive in the dynamic and ever-evolving game development industry.

Section 20.3: Finding Employment in the Gaming Industry

While freelancing and contract work provide flexibility and independence, many game developers aspire to secure full-time employment within established game development companies. In this section, we'll explore the process of finding employment in the gaming industry, including strategies for job hunting, building a strong resume, and excelling in interviews.

1. Preparing for Employment

Before applying for game development positions, it's essential to have the necessary skills and qualifications. Many game development roles require expertise in programming languages like C++, C#, or JavaScript, as well as proficiency in game engines and development tools such as Unity or Unreal Engine. Consider obtaining relevant certifications or completing formal education programs if necessary.

2. Building a Strong Resume and Portfolio

A well-crafted resume and portfolio are your key tools for impressing potential employers. Your resume should highlight your skills, experience, and achievements in the game development field. Include details about the games you've worked on, your role, and any significant contributions. Your portfolio should showcase your best work, including game projects, code samples, and visual assets.

3. Job Search Strategies

Finding job openings in the gaming industry requires active job searching. Use online job boards, company websites, and professional networking platforms like LinkedIn to identify job opportunities. Consider attending job fairs, gaming conferences, and industry events to network with potential employers and learn about job openings.

4. Tailoring Your Application

Each job application should be tailored to the specific position and company you're applying to. Customize your resume and cover letter to match the requirements and culture of the target company. Highlight relevant skills and experiences that make you a strong fit for the role.

5. Preparing for Interviews

Interviews for game development positions often include technical assessments and portfolio reviews. Practice coding challenges and be ready to discuss your past projects in detail. Prepare for both technical and behavioral interview questions, showcasing your problem-solving abilities, teamwork, and passion for game development.

6. Showcasing Your Skills

During interviews, demonstrate your skills and passion for game development. If applicable, bring a portfolio of your work or be prepared to walk through code samples. Show a deep understanding of game mechanics, design principles, and the specific role you're applying for.

7. Company Culture Fit

Employers often assess whether candidates will fit well into their company culture. Research the company's values, work environment, and projects. Be prepared to discuss how your personality and work style align with their culture.

8. Networking and Referrals

Networking is a valuable tool for finding job opportunities in the gaming industry. Connect with professionals in the field, attend industry events, and consider reaching out to current employees at companies you're interested in. Referrals from within the industry can lead to job openings that may not be publicly advertised.

9. Internships and Entry-Level Positions

Consider starting your career with internships or entry-level positions, even if they are not your dream role. These opportunities provide valuable experience and connections within the industry, making it easier to move into more senior roles in the future.

10. Continuous Learning

Game development is a continuously evolving field. Stay up-to-date with the latest technologies, trends, and tools by pursuing online courses, attending workshops, and participating in game development communities. Continuous learning demonstrates your commitment to professional growth.

11. Patience and Persistence

Finding a job in the gaming industry can be competitive, so patience and persistence are essential. Don't get discouraged by rejections; use them as opportunities for self-improvement and refinement of your job-seeking strategies.

12. Conclusion

Securing employment in the gaming industry is achievable with the right combination of skills, networking, and determination. By preparing thoroughly, tailoring your applications, and demonstrating your passion for game development, you can increase your chances of landing your desired role in the dynamic and exciting world of game development.

Section 20.4: Networking and Community Involvement

Building a successful career in game development extends beyond technical skills and employment opportunities. Networking and active involvement in the game development community play a pivotal role in fostering growth, learning, and collaboration. In this section, we'll explore the significance of networking and community engagement in the gaming industry.

1. Why Networking Matters

Networking is the process of establishing and nurturing relationships within the gaming industry. It encompasses interactions with fellow developers, industry professionals, and potential employers. Networking offers several advantages:

- **Opportunities:** Networking can lead to job opportunities, collaborations on projects, and access to valuable resources.
- **Learning:** Engaging with experienced developers allows you to learn from their insights, experiences, and expertise.
- **Support:** The gaming community provides a support system for sharing knowledge, solving problems, and overcoming challenges.
- **Visibility:** Building a network can increase your visibility and reputation in the industry, potentially leading to more opportunities.

2. Where to Network

Networking opportunities are abundant in the gaming industry. Here are some places and platforms where you can start building your network:

- **Gaming Conferences and Expos:** Attend industry events like GDC (Game Developers Conference), E3, or PAX to meet professionals and showcase your work.
- **Online Forums and Communities:** Join game development forums, Reddit communities, and Discord servers related to your interests.
- **Social Media:** Platforms like Twitter, LinkedIn, and Instagram allow you to connect with professionals and share your work.
- **Local Meetups and Dev Groups:** Look for game development meetups, hackathons, or developer groups in your area.
- **Game Jams:** Participate in game jams to collaborate with others and showcase your skills.
- **Online Courses and Webinars:** Attend webinars and online courses to learn from experts and connect with fellow students.

3. Building Meaningful Connections

Effective networking involves more than just collecting contacts. Here are some tips for building meaningful connections:

- **Be Genuine:** Approach networking with authenticity. Be yourself and show a genuine interest in others' work and experiences.
- **Offer Value:** Provide value to your connections by sharing your knowledge, insights, or resources when appropriate.
- **Ask Questions:** Asking questions and showing curiosity can lead to meaningful conversations and connections.
- **Follow Up:** After meeting someone, follow up with a friendly message or email to maintain the connection.
- **Stay Active:** Consistently engage with your network, whether through online discussions, sharing updates, or attending events.

4. Collaboration and Projects

Networking often leads to collaboration on game projects. Working with others can help you gain new skills, expand your portfolio, and build lasting relationships. Collaborative projects can range from small indie games to larger commercial ventures. Be open to opportunities and explore projects that align with your interests and goals.

5. Giving Back to the Community

As you grow in your career, consider giving back to the community. Mentorship, sharing knowledge, and assisting newcomers can be incredibly rewarding. Contributing to open-source projects, creating tutorials, or speaking at industry events can help you establish yourself as a valuable member of the gaming community.

6. Conclusion

Networking and community involvement are integral aspects of a successful game development career. By actively engaging with others, sharing your passion, and building meaningful connections, you can navigate the gaming industry with greater ease, continuously expand your knowledge, and contribute to the vibrant and collaborative world of game development.

Section 20.5: Continuing Education and Skill Development

In the ever-evolving field of game development, staying up-to-date with the latest technologies, tools, and trends is essential for a successful career. Section 20.5 explores the importance of continuing education and skill development in the world of game development.

1. Lifelong Learning

The world of technology is constantly changing, and game development is no exception. New programming languages, frameworks, and design principles emerge regularly. To remain competitive and adaptable, it's crucial to adopt a mindset of lifelong learning. Here's how you can approach it:

- **Online Courses and Tutorials:** Platforms like Udemy, Coursera, and Pluralsight offer a wide range of game development courses, from beginner to advanced levels.
- **Game Development Blogs and Websites:** Stay updated with industry news, tutorials, and best practices by following blogs and websites dedicated to game development.
- **Books and Publications:** Invest in books and publications that cover the latest developments in game design, programming, and game art.
- **Game Jams and Hackathons:** Participate in game jams and hackathons to challenge yourself and acquire new skills in a short timeframe.
- **Online Communities:** Engage with online communities and forums to seek advice, share knowledge, and collaborate on projects.

2. Specialization and Expertise

As you progress in your career, consider specializing in a particular area of game development that aligns with your interests and strengths. Specialization allows you to become an expert in a specific field, such as gameplay programming, 3D modeling, or narrative design. Expertise can lead to more exciting job opportunities and increased demand for your skills.

3. Game Development Tools and Software

Familiarize yourself with the latest game development tools and software. Industry-standard tools like Unity, Unreal Engine, and Godot continue to evolve, offering new features and improvements. Keep your skills sharp by exploring these tools and experimenting with their capabilities.

4. Attending Workshops and Conferences

Game development workshops and conferences provide opportunities to learn from experts, network with industry professionals, and gain insights into emerging technologies. Events like GDC, SIGGRAPH, and local game developer meetups offer valuable educational experiences.

5. Online Learning Communities

Online communities, such as Stack Overflow, GitHub, and Discord servers, are excellent places to collaborate, share knowledge, and seek guidance. Active participation in these communities can help you solve problems, receive feedback on your projects, and connect with mentors.

6. Personal Projects and Experimentation

One of the most effective ways to develop your skills is through personal projects and experimentation. Create your own games, explore new game mechanics, or build innovative tools. These projects not only serve as a learning experience but also enhance your portfolio and demonstrate your abilities to potential employers.

7. Networking for Learning

Networking isn't just about finding job opportunities; it's also about finding mentors and learning from experienced professionals. Forge relationships with individuals who can guide you in your career and offer valuable insights and advice.

8. Certifications and Degrees

Consider pursuing certifications or degrees in game development or related fields. Formal education can provide you with a strong foundation and industry-recognized qualifications. Many universities and online institutions offer degree programs tailored to game development.

9. Conclusion

Continuing education and skill development are integral to a successful and fulfilling career in game development. Embrace a growth mindset, seek out learning opportunities, and adapt to industry changes. By investing in your education and continuously honing your skills, you'll be well-prepared to tackle the exciting challenges and innovations that await in the world of game development.